AF479023

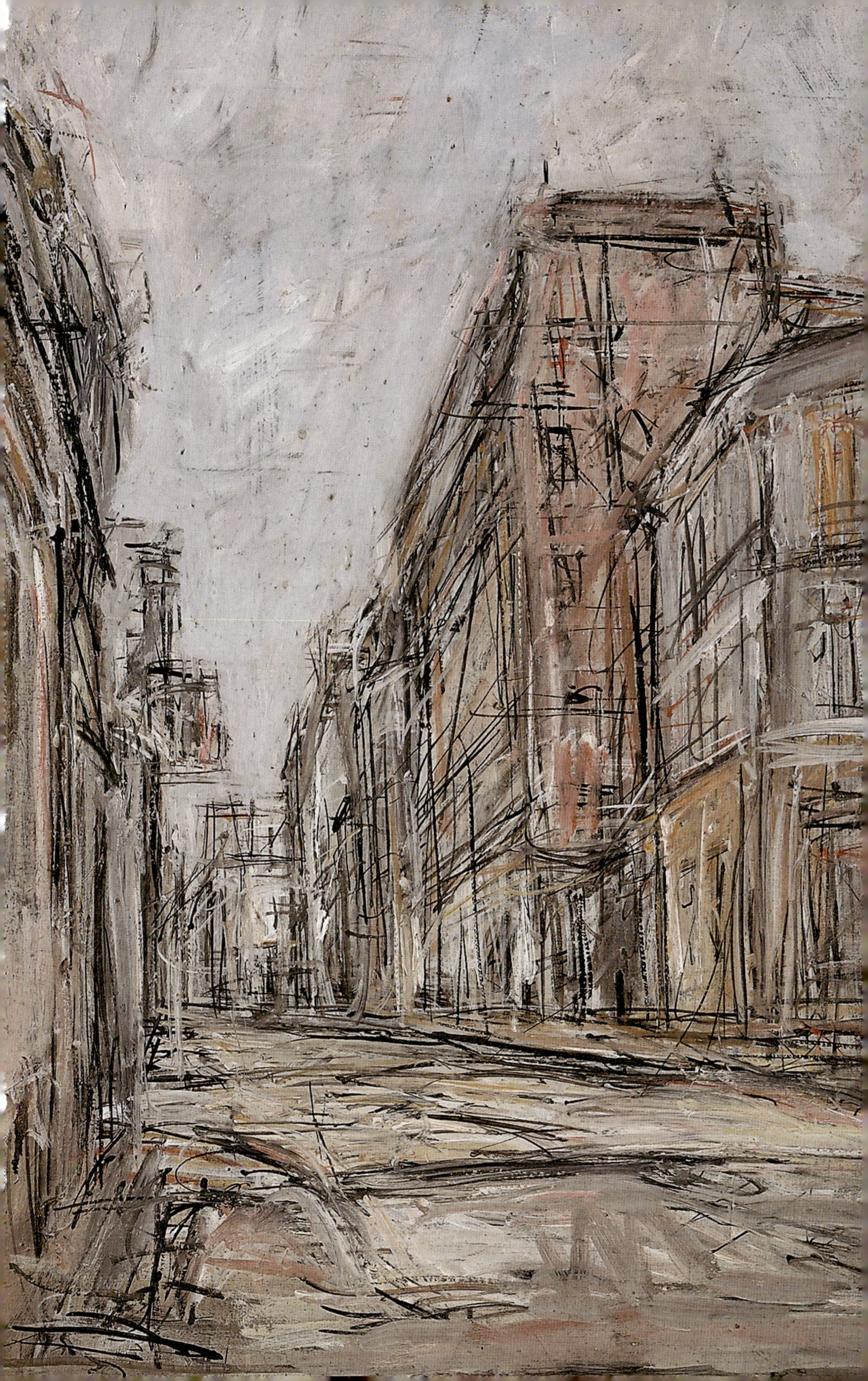

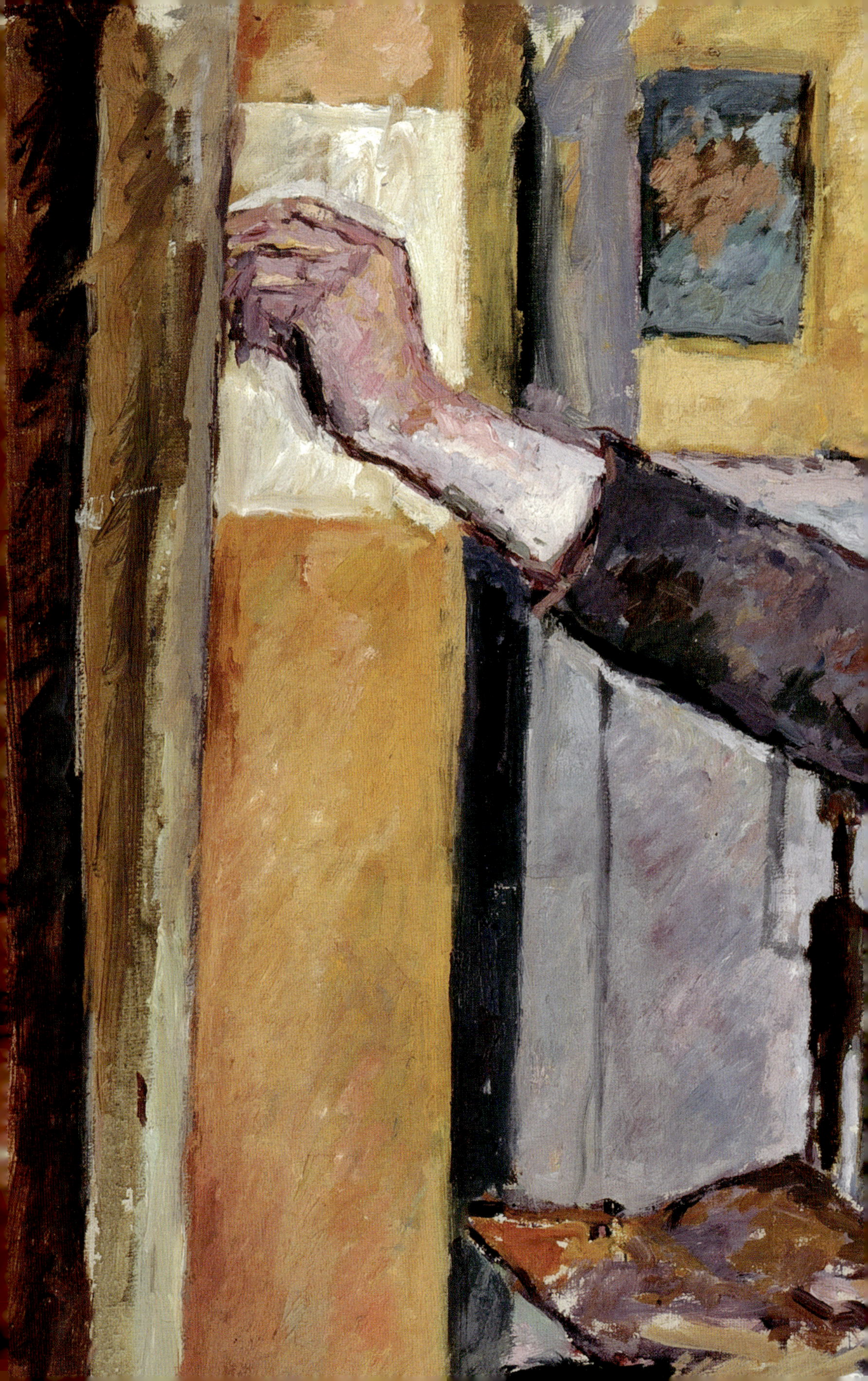

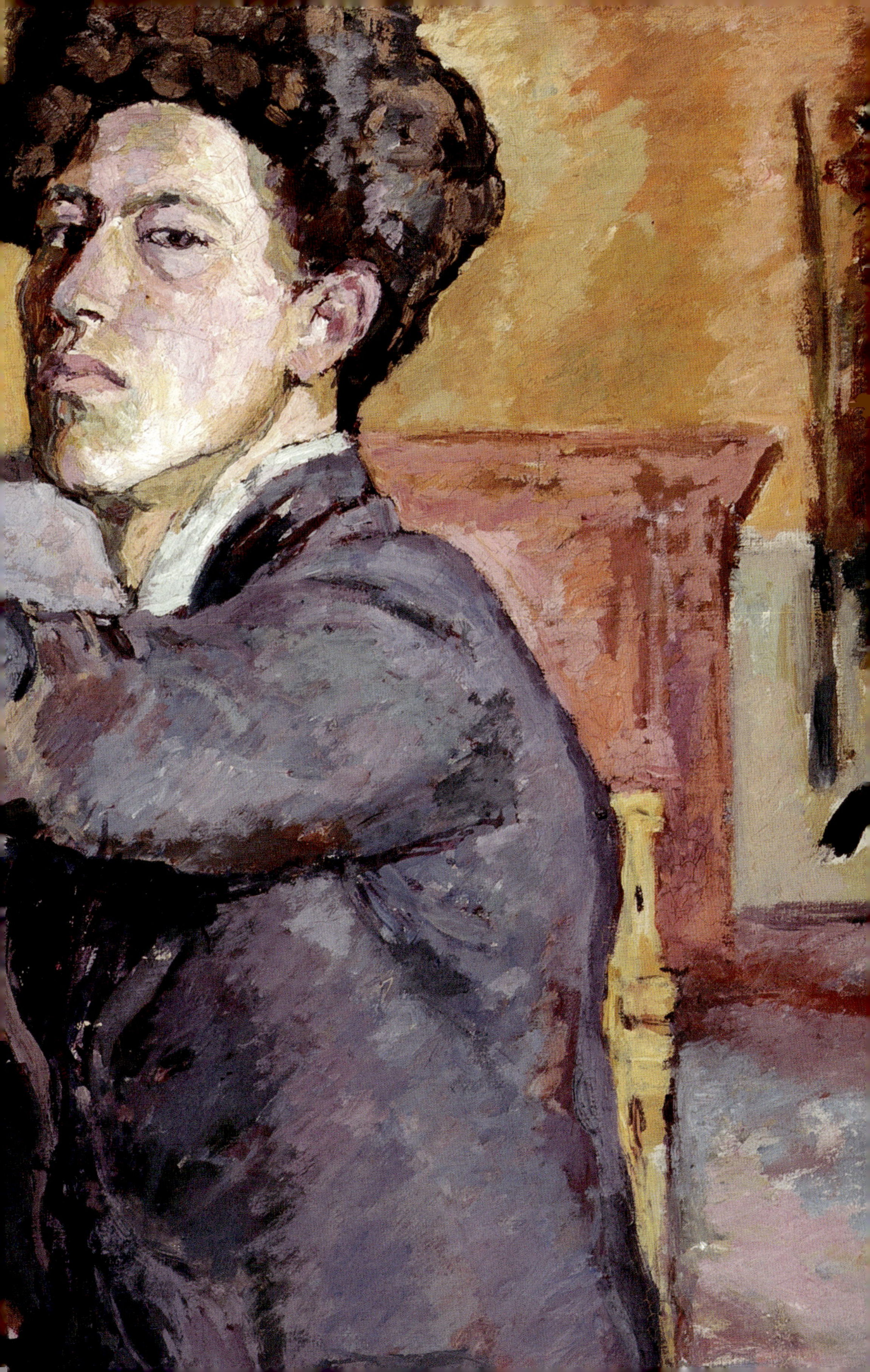

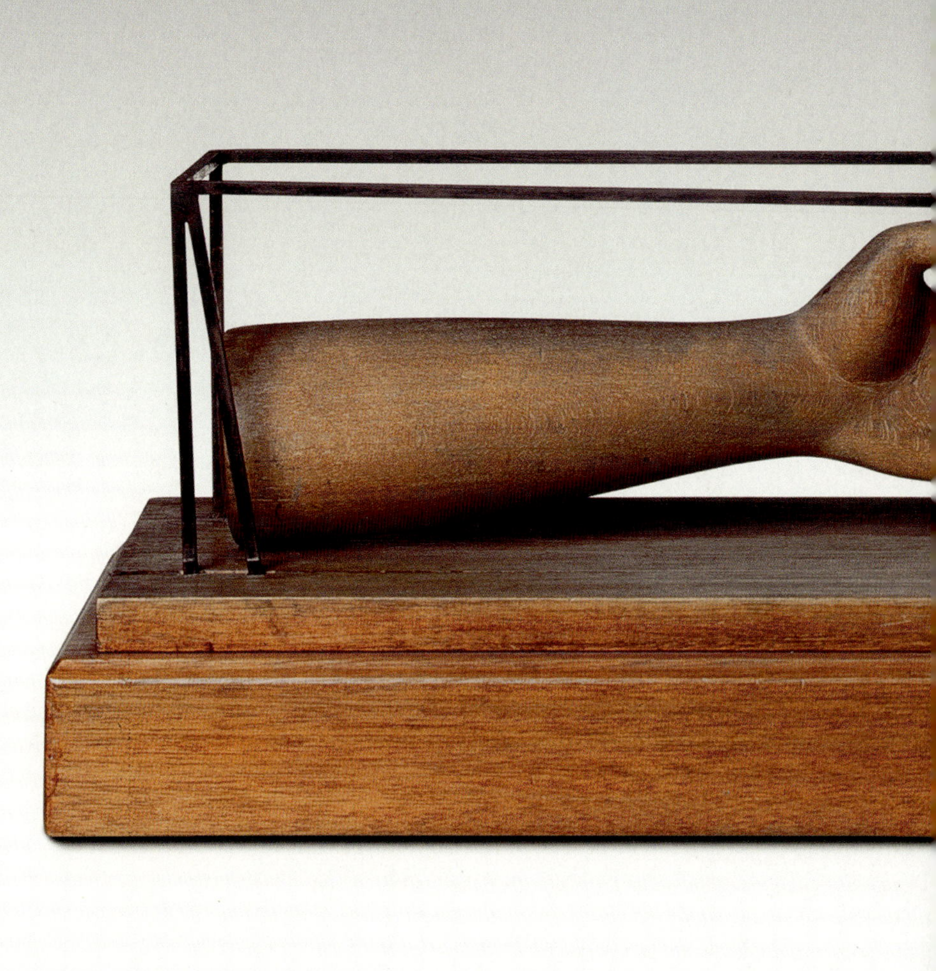

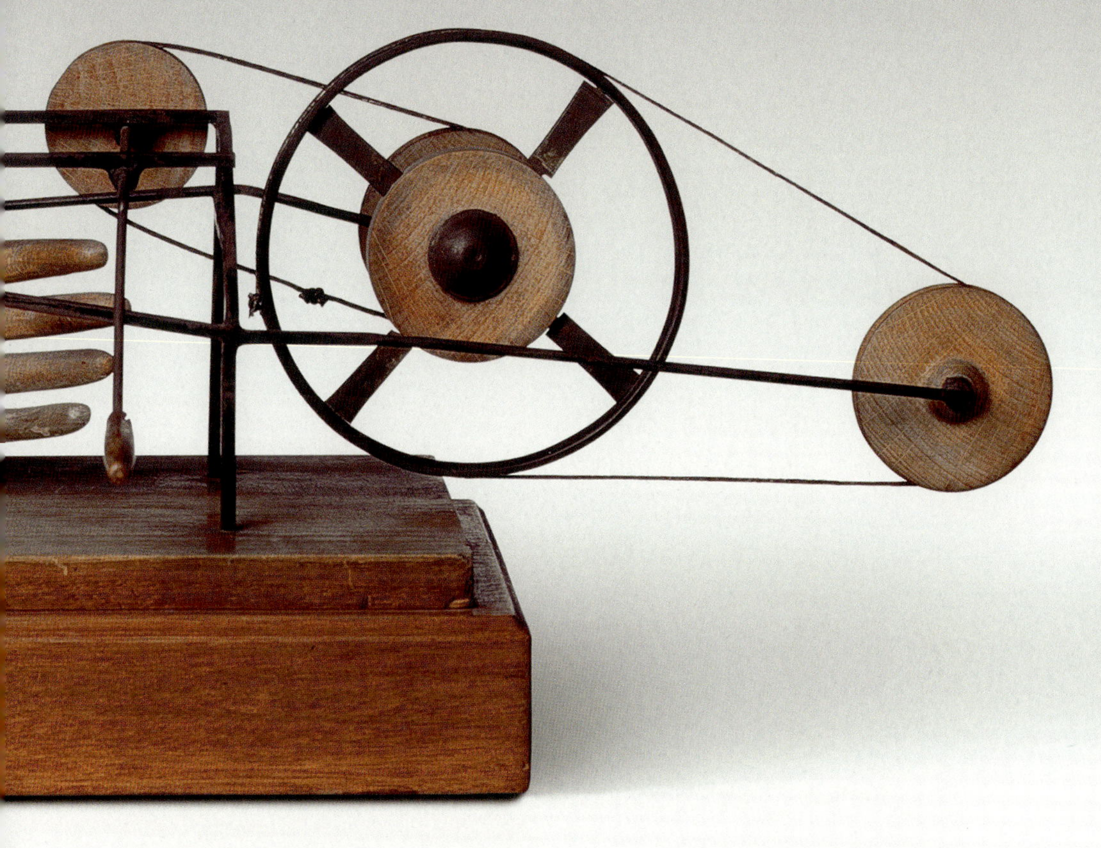

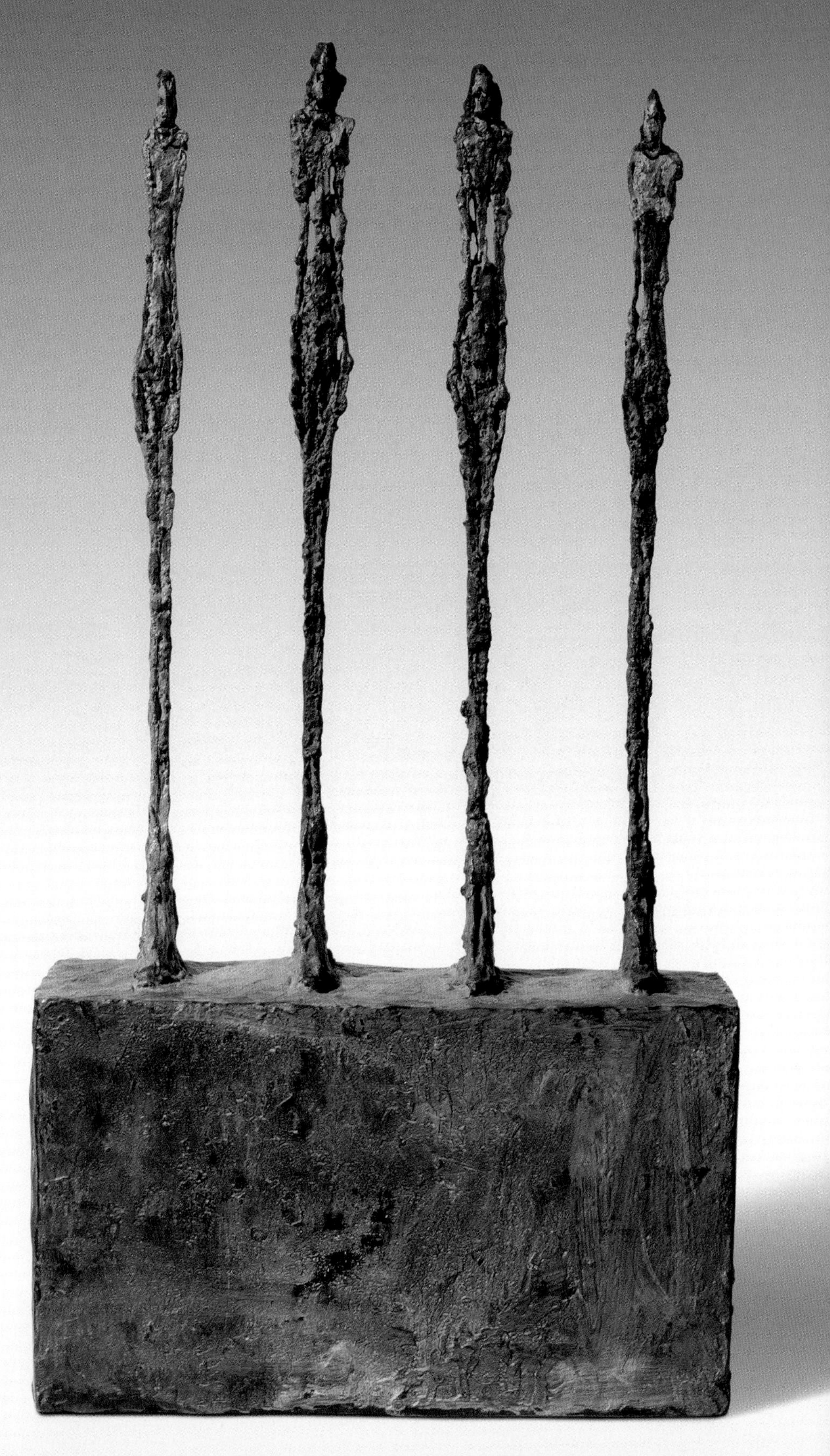

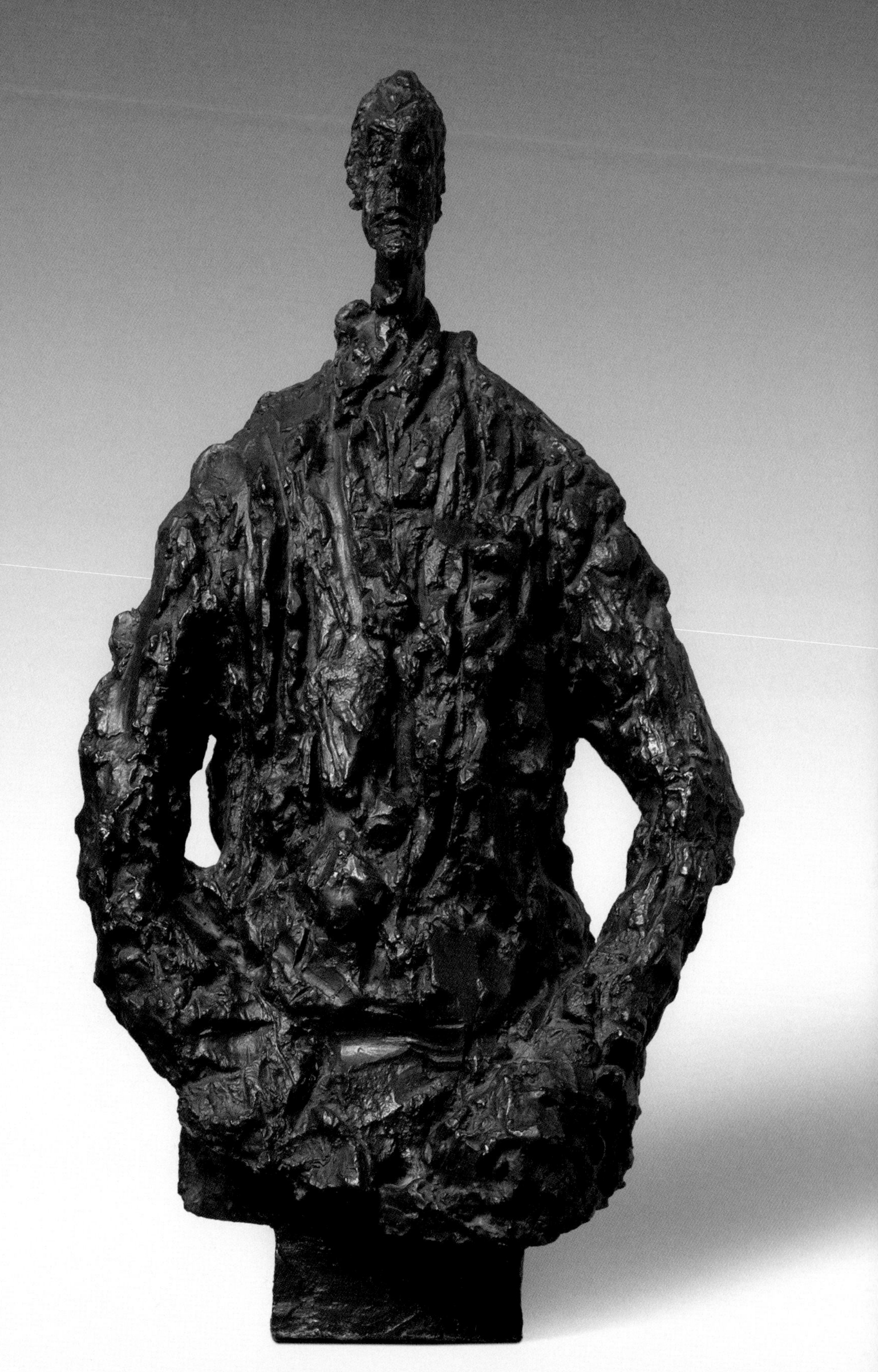

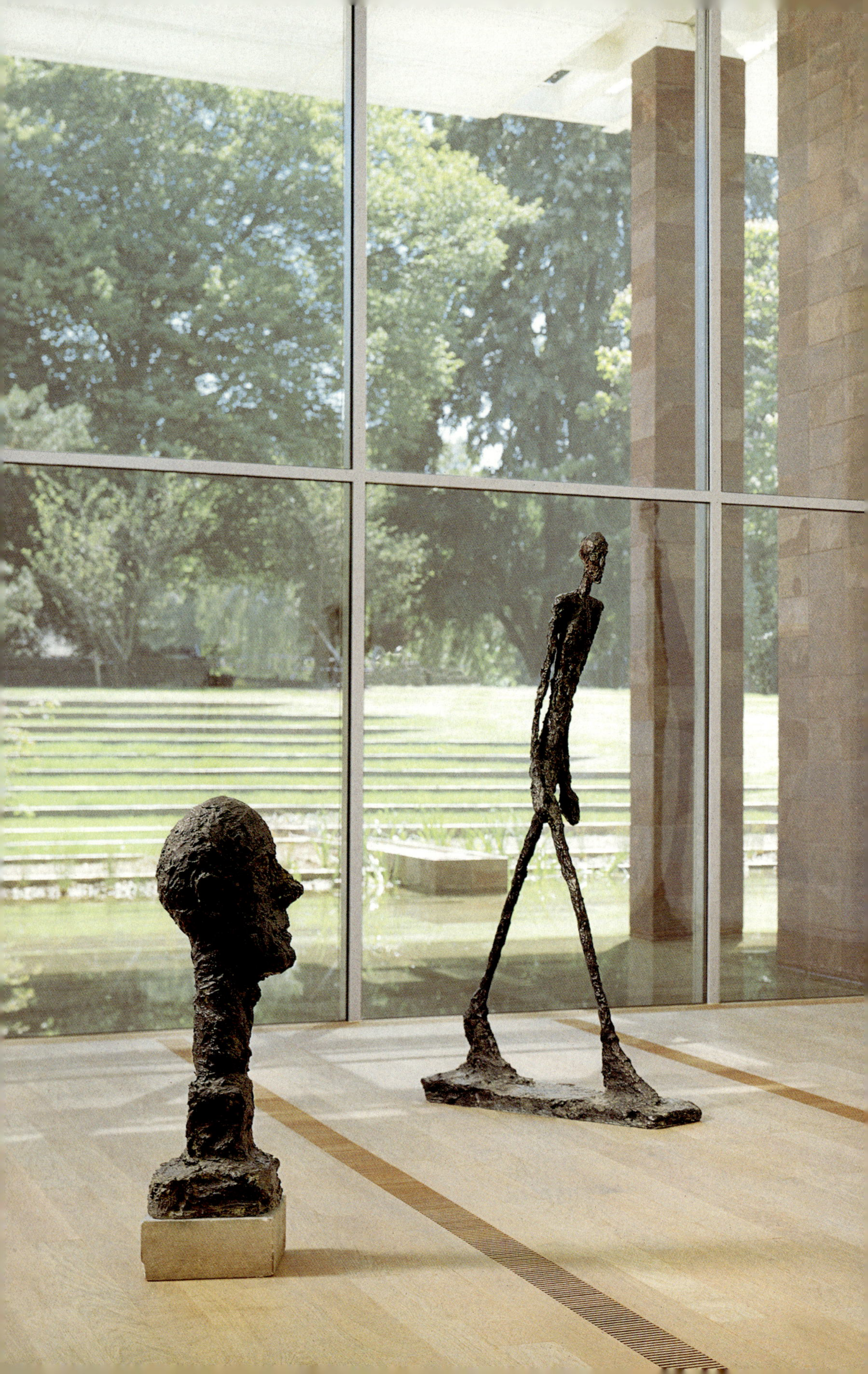

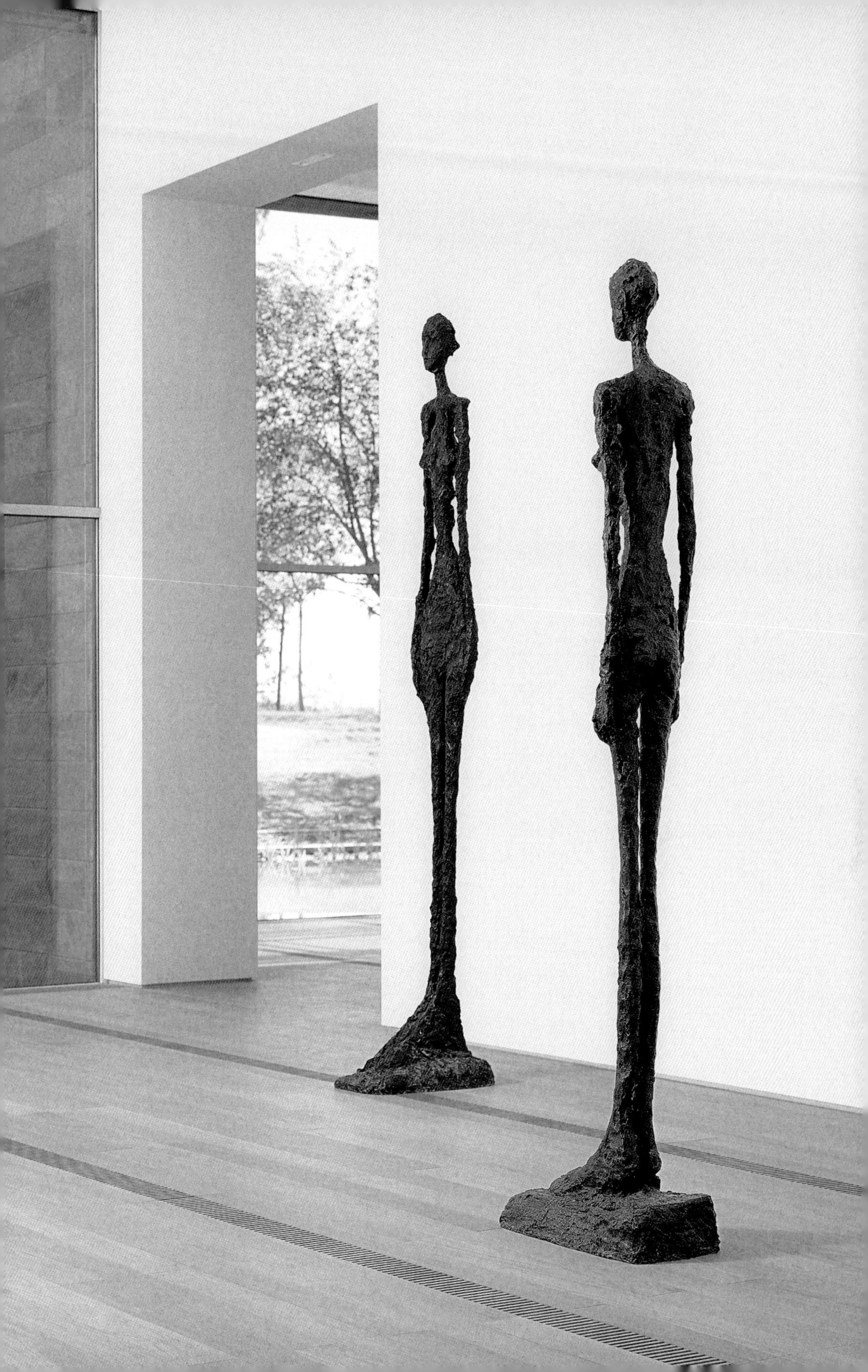

Ulf Küster

Alberto Giacometti: Space, Figure, Time

© **2009** Hatje Cantz Verlag, Ostfildern, and author © **2009** for the reproduced works by Alberto Giacometti: Succession Giacometti / VG Bild-Kunst, Bonn **Published by** Hatje Cantz Verlag, Zeppelinstrasse 32, 73760 Ostfildern, Germany, Telephone +49 711 4405-200, Fax +49 711 4405-220. Hatje Cantz books are available internationally at selected bookstores. For more information about our distribution partners, please visit our homepage at www.hatjecantz.com **Copyediting:** Melanie Eckner **Translations:** Michael Wolfson **Graphic design and typesetting:** Margarethe Hausstätter **Production:** Christine Emter, Hatje Cantz **Reproductions**: hausstætter herstellung, Berlin **Typeface:** Augerau, Conduit **Paper:** LuxoSamtoffset, 135 g/m² **Printing and binding:** fgb freiburger graphische betriebe **ISBN 978-3-7757-2373-2** (Englisch) **ISBN 978-3-7757-2372-5** (German) **Printed in Germany**

Front cover: Alberto Giacometti drawing **Back cover:** *Homme qui marche II (Walking Man II)*, 1960, Fondation Beyeler, Riehen / Basel **Page 1:** *La Rue (The Street in front of the Studio)*, 1952, Fondation Beyeler, Riehen / Basel **Pages 2/3:** *Self-Portrait* (detail), 1921, Alberto Giacometti Foundation, Zurich **Pages 4/5:** *Main prise (Caught Hand)*, 1932, Alberto Giacometti Foundation, Zurich **Page 6:** *Quatre Femmes sur socle (Four Women on a Base)*, 1950, Alberto Giacometti Foundation, Zurich, on permanent loan to the Kunstmuseum Basel **Page 7:** *Diego au chandail (Diego in a Sweater)*, 1953, Alberto Giacometti Foundation, Zurich **Pages 8/9:** Sculptural group for Chase Manhattan Plaza, New York *(Standing Woman III and IV, Monumental Head, Walking Man II)*, 1960, Fondation Beyeler, Riehen / Basel **Pages 11, 12:** Sculptures and wall drawings in the Parisian studio (details)

ULF KÜSTER

ALBERTO GIACOMETTI

SPACE, FIGURE, TIME

HATJE CANTZ

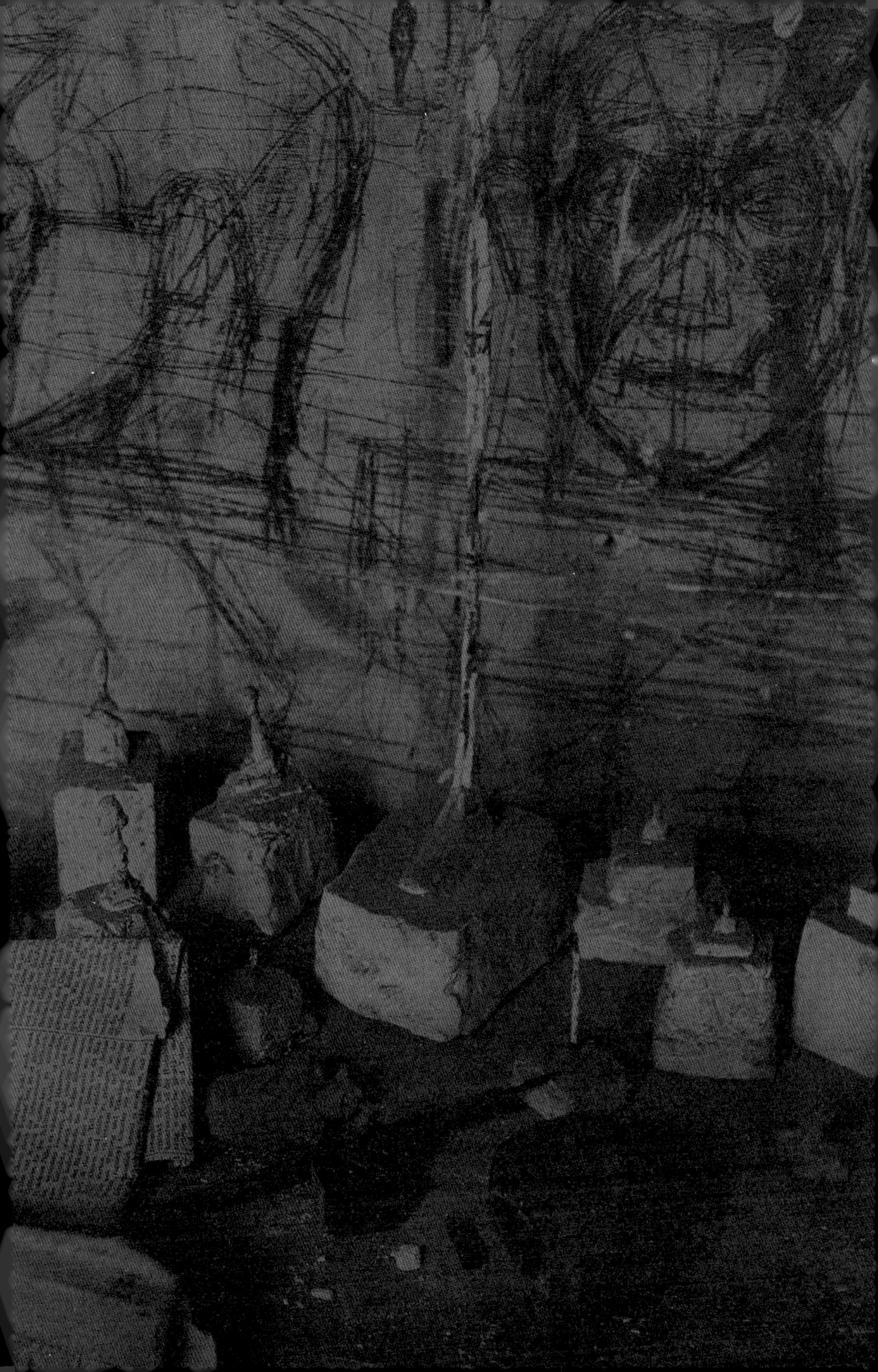

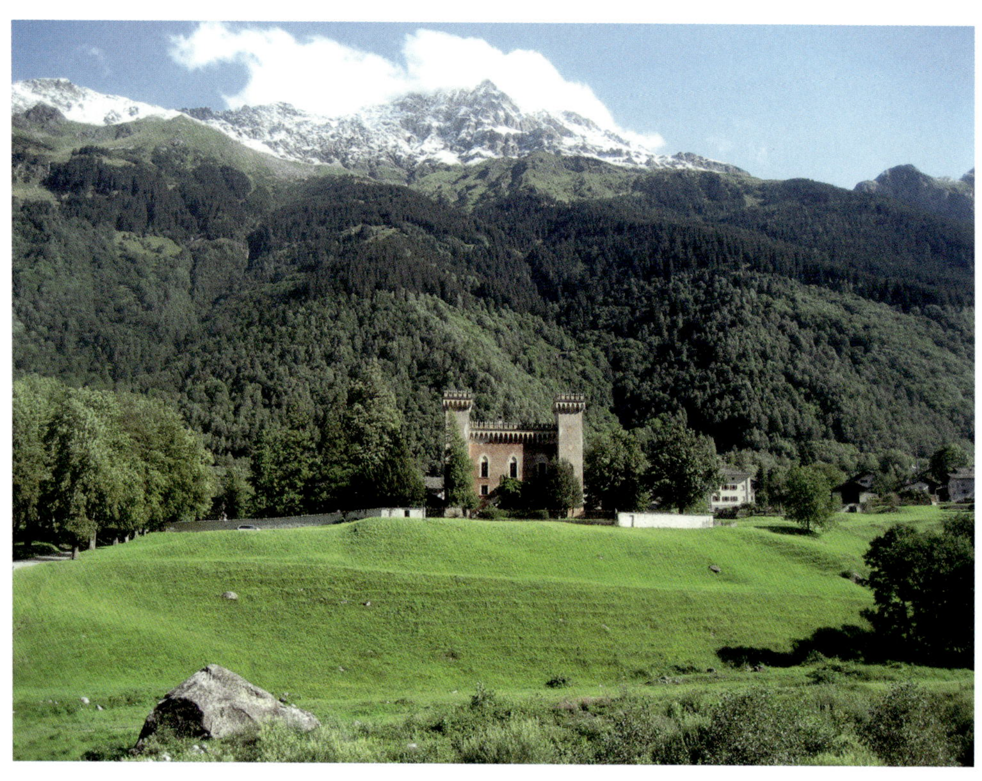

Palazzo Castelmur in Coltura
near Stampa with the Piz Duan
in the background, 2008

Alberto Giacometti's friend of many years, the photographer and publisher Ernst Scheidegger, had warned: you can expect snow on the Julier Pass even at the height of summer. To reach Val Bregaglia, the native region of the Giacometti family, from northern Switzerland, one must choose this route and cross the mountain chain that seems to separate the plateau including Lake Sils from the rest of the world. Scheidegger was right. A blizzard with rain and snow wailed over the Julier Pass—down towards Maloja, through the narrow bends to the solitude of Val Bregaglia and Stampa.

After a storm-drenched night in Stampa in which it seemed as if air masses had thundered down from mountains into the valley, the morning was fresh and clear: radiant sunshine and majestic high summits all round. In pursuit of remembrances of Alberto Giacometti (1901–1966) one first encounters the birthplace, marked with a plaque, of the painter Augusto Giacometti, a distant uncle of Alberto's. The birthplace of Alberto's father Giovanni Giacometti, also a famous painter, is the former Piz Duan inn, likewise adorned with a plaque. It stands at the bridge over the Mera River, which, depending on the season, is a more or less torrential mountain stream that flows past Stampa along the road from Maloja to Italy. Directly opposite it, on the main street, stands the home into which Giovanni's family moved in 1906, along with the stables that were converted into the studio used by father and son. There is no plaque here, but it is nevertheless well-known from Ernst Scheidegger's photographs. This is the place where Alberto grew up. He and his father worked here, and Alberto regularly returned here from cosmopolitan Paris until his death. Of all the places of remembrance we know, this is one of the most spectacular because of the mountain scenery, but also one of the most prosaic: many villages in the Swiss Alpine valleys also look like this.

The celebrated members of the Giacometti family are honored in a special room in the late sixteenth-century "Ciäsa Granda," now the regional museum of local history, where works by Alberto can also be found. These include the sculpture *Elie Lotar III* that he left behind in his Parisian studio before his death and which his brother Diego had cast. It originally stood on his grave, but it was later given a permanent place here after being stolen and then recovered. But the introduction to the region's natural history, packed to the rafters with its depiction of Val Bregaglia's fauna, seems even more impressive. One now has the slightly sobering, but at the same time comforting feeling that nature, and not art, is what matters most. Perhaps the best place to encounter the spirits of the town's illustrious dead is the municipal cemetery that lies somewhat uphill near Borgonovo, Alberto's true birthplace where his family lived before moving to Stampa.

They are all united there with one exception: Alberto's wife Annette Giacometti, née Arm, is not buried here. But Giovanni Giacometti (1868–1933) rests here with his wife Annetta, née Stampa (1871–1964), the famous "Mamma a Stampa," under a gravestone designed by Alberto. Odette Giacometti (1910–2007) also rests in peace there, the wife of Bruno Giacometti, who was born in 1907 as the youngest child of Annetta and Giovanni and is now the last survivor of the family. The gravestone of Alberto himself is not far away. In accordance with Jewish custom, small stones have been placed on it, a sign that he is revered across all national and religious boundaries. Behind Alberto, in the cemetery wall, is the stone for his brother Diego (1902–1985). Nearby, also set in the wall, is the tablet in memory of his sister Ottilia (1904–1937), her husband Francis Berthoud (1894–1959), and her son Silvio Berthoud (1937–1991), at whose birth she died. The exact dates of birth and death are also interesting. Like his uncle Alberto, Silvio was born on October 10. Ottilia died on October 11, and October 12 was the birthday of Francis Berthoud, who died on May 31, his wife's birthday.

At the furthermost corner of the cemetery, far removed from the other Giacomettis, a large funerary monument stands on the grave of the painter Augusto Giacometti (1877–1947), the *maestro dei colori* who truly deserved this honorary title. His picture depicting the angel and the three Marys at the sepulchre of Christ in the lunette above the choir has dominated the Church of San Pietro at Coltura near Stampa since 1915, and the lunette above the choir in the Church of San Giorgio next to the cemetery in Borgonovo has been adorned since 1935 with one of his famous stained glass windows:

16

Christ's Entrance into Jerusalem. Churchgoers from the area therefore often saw works by Augusto Giacometti in the first half of the twentieth century. He must have long been more popular in the valley than Giovanni and naturally more popular than Alberto as well.

And the other gravestones—numerous Giacomettis, the Stampas they were related to, the Baldinis and so forth; all honorable residents of Val Bregaglia. The name Giacometti is common in this area; the family must be very large with many branches. Large families mean large problems and animosities. Bruno Giacometti responded to the question about his family's relationship to Augusto Giacometti by saying: You said "Grüezi" (hello) to one another when you ran into him in the buffet at Zurich train station, something that happened every once in a while because Augusto lived in Zurich and Giovanni regularly exhibited there, but you didn't then sit down together at the same table. . . . This was by no means meant to be understood as a reflection on Augusto as an artist, but alludes instead to family differences about which they still speak in Stampa today, even though possibly nobody knows the reasons why any longer.

It must be emphasized that the view from the cemetery goes off into the *expanse* of the valley: the expanse, not the narrowness, as one often reads. Naturally this valley is deeply indented and surrounded on all sides by chains of high mountains. And naturally it was, and still is, a problem that not a single ray of sunshine reaches the valley floor during three months in winter (which is not particularly unusual in Alpine valleys), but one rarely has a feeling of constriction in the valley itself. And it is worth asking whether the valley's special light conditions, which not only result from its depths, but also from its northeasterly to southwesterly orientation, are particularly favorable for painters? Even so, the valley brought forth two great colorists in Giovanni and Augusto Giacometti, and Alberto Giacometti, who was something of an anti-colorist, explained the dominance of the color gray so characteristic of his pictures, which can be associated with the lightless winter months in Val Bregaglia, by saying that it represented all colors for him.

The name Giacometti
represents
modern Switzerland.

Or was it not only the light conditions, but rather some other factors that produced so many talented artists? Probably: the isolation of the valley felt by travelers coming through the passes and summer snow

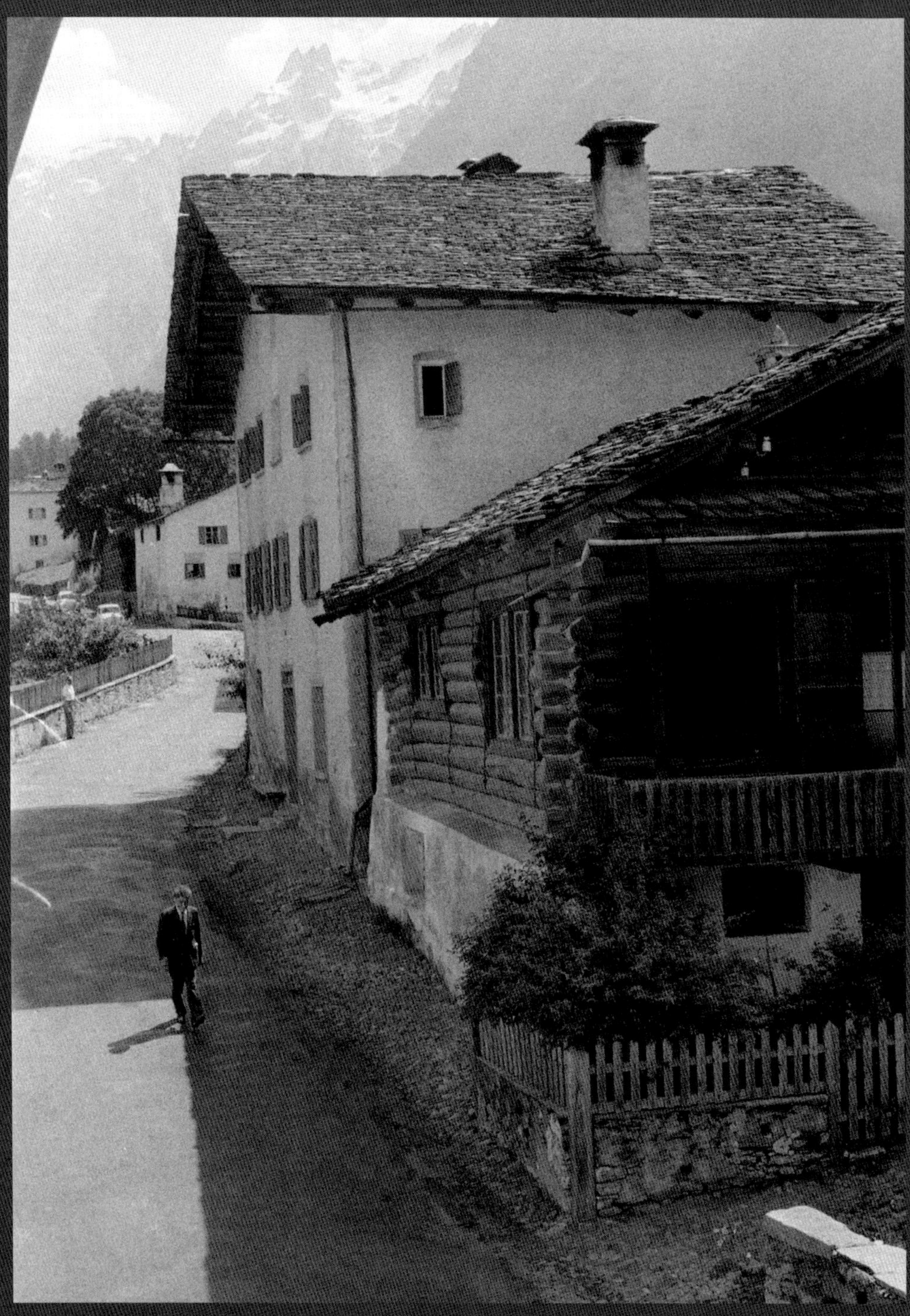

Alberto Giacometti in front of his
parental home and the studio in Stampa, 1950s

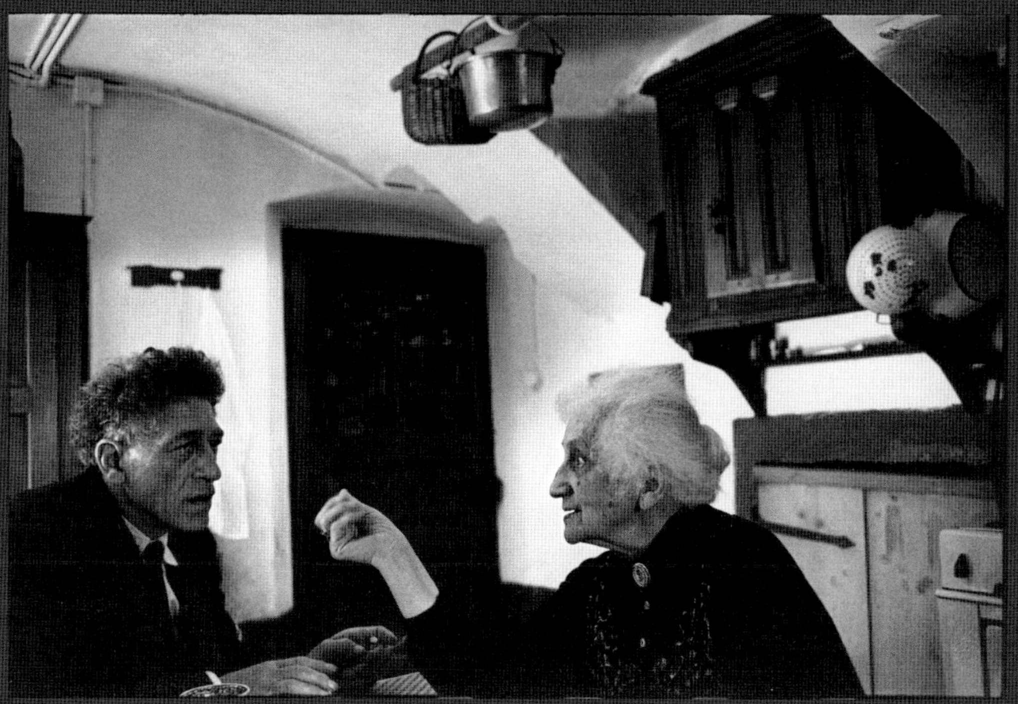

Alberto with his mother in Stampa, 1961
Photographed by Henri Cartier-Bresson

whereby she naturally had the paintings by her deceased husband as shining examples in mind. Alberto would then apologetically respond that he tried as best he could to do so, but they were as gray as always when he finished painting them and he could not understand why. This anecdote was recounted by Ernst Beyeler. Sons always remain sons for their mothers, even though they might have become world famous in the meanwhile.

In any case, Annetta was a devoted artist's wife who wholeheartedly supported her husband. She believed in the artist in her husband. This belief, which could possibly have meant sacrifice and deprivation, might seem somewhat old-fashioned today. But it was a defining experience for Alberto. His future wife Annette subordinated herself just as unconditionally, at least during the first years of their relationship and marriage. The fact that he tied himself at all may well have resulted from the fact that he saw in her a woman who would support him in the way he saw his mother support his father. The artist—that is, primarily the father and soon Alberto as well—played a special role in this family. Not only the mother, but also the siblings, especially Diego, who always placed himself in the background, accepted this.

"I cannot imagine
a happier childhood . . ."

The marriage between Annetta and Giovanni celebrated on October 4, 1900, seems to have been a very happy one. The couple had four children: Alberto, born on October 10, 1901; Diego, born on November 15, 1902; Ottilia, born on May 31, 1904; and Bruno, born on August 24, 1907. Looking at the early family photographs, for example those taken by Gertrud Dübi-Müller in 1911, or the pictures of the family gathered at the dining table in Stampa that probably date from 1906–07 (ill. page 25), one gets the impression of an completely "modern" family in which the parents were undoubtedly respected, but in which the children's talents were also permitted to unfold. A letter written by Annetta to Anna Amiet on December 25, 1908, illustrates how life was in the Giacometti family. Anna Amiet was the wife of the painter Cuno Amiet (1868–1961), Giovanni's lifelong friend and confidant as well as Alberto's godfather. While it is noticeable from Annetta's letter that German was not her everyday means of communication, she could certainly express herself very well in it. This too, the polyglot, is a sign of the Giacometti family's worldliness, and they are by no means an isolated case in Switzerland:

24

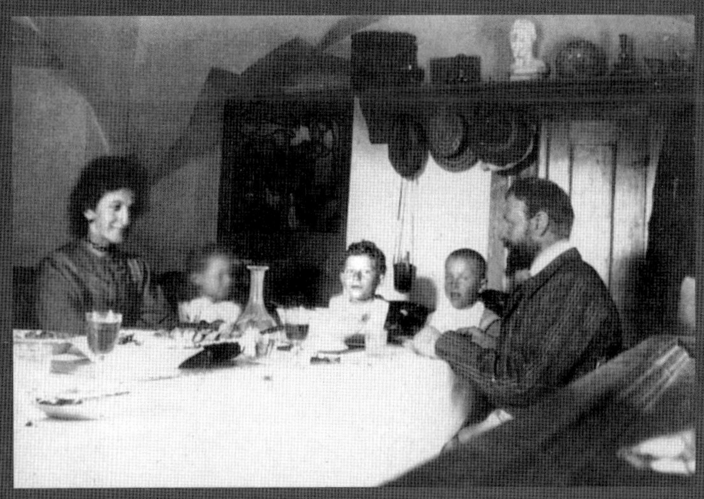

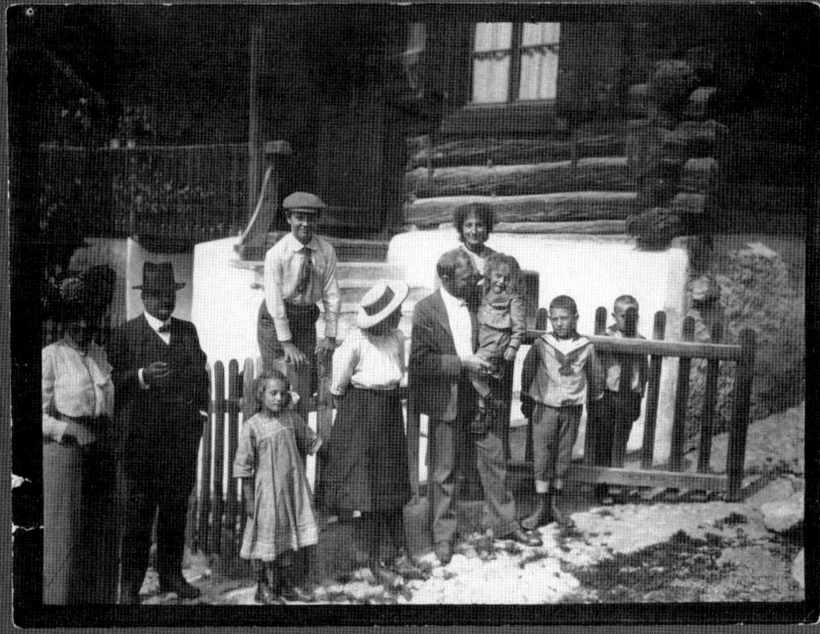

The Giacometti family
at the dining table, ca. 1906–07
From left to right:
Annetta, Ottilia, Alberto, Diego, and Giovanni

The family with friends, ca. 1910
Bruno is in his father's arms, Alberto is to the
right of him, Ottilia is at the left
without a hat, Annetta is in the background,
Diego is partially hidden by the fence.

"Alberto likes going to school very much; he blissfully learns to read and write, is very dexterous in arithmetic, and delights in drawing; as far as singing is concerned, he is unfortunately also is father's son.—Brunetto was not well recently and was therefore spoiled by everyone; he has now turned into a little tyrant. Very much like Alberto at that age, he is infatuated with his father and screams every time Giovanin leaves the room. But I get my turn at night. He will hopefully get better soon; I will then catch up on lost sleep! Diego and Ottilia are almost always outside. They had much pleasure in the Christmas tree; there was much to talk and argue about today and so the time passes."[5]

"I could not imagine a happier childhood than the one I spent with my father and my whole family—mother, sister, and brothers," Alberto summed up in a letter to Peter F. Althaus published in the March 1958 issue of the magazine *Du*. Artistically, all the members of his family were important; they all sat for him. At the same time it is certain that solely the presence of his parents and siblings as models had a similar, if not even greater value for Alberto than did their own artistic production. And what was Alberto's relationship to his siblings like?

Diego Giacometti—whose Christian name is supposed to be his father's homage to Diego Velázquez, while Alberto's name not only honors his grandfather but also Albrecht Dürer—was only thirteen months younger than his brother. As his father wrote to his friend Cuno Amiet on the day after Diego's birth, Alberto was enthusiastic about his little brother and already wanted to give him "a book to browse through."[6] The father's remark shows that Alberto even then instinctively saw his brother as someone to whom he could pass along his knowledge and with whom he could share his secrets—typical behavior for a first-born child and a highly talented one as well. While Diego developed completely differently than Alberto, and he surely suffered under the domination of his ingenious brother, the relationship between the two of them was nevertheless very close. When the two brothers were living together in Paris, they spoke to each other in the Italian dialect of Val Bregaglia, a language only they understood. And for this reason alone, they formed a kind of conspiratorial clan.

In March 1907, Diego's right hand was maimed in a chaffcutter—a catastrophe in a family fixated on working with one's hands. It is nothing less than remarkable that Diego nevertheless had a career as a craftsman and artist. Throughout his life, he made light of his disability; he later characterized the incident to Alberto's biog-

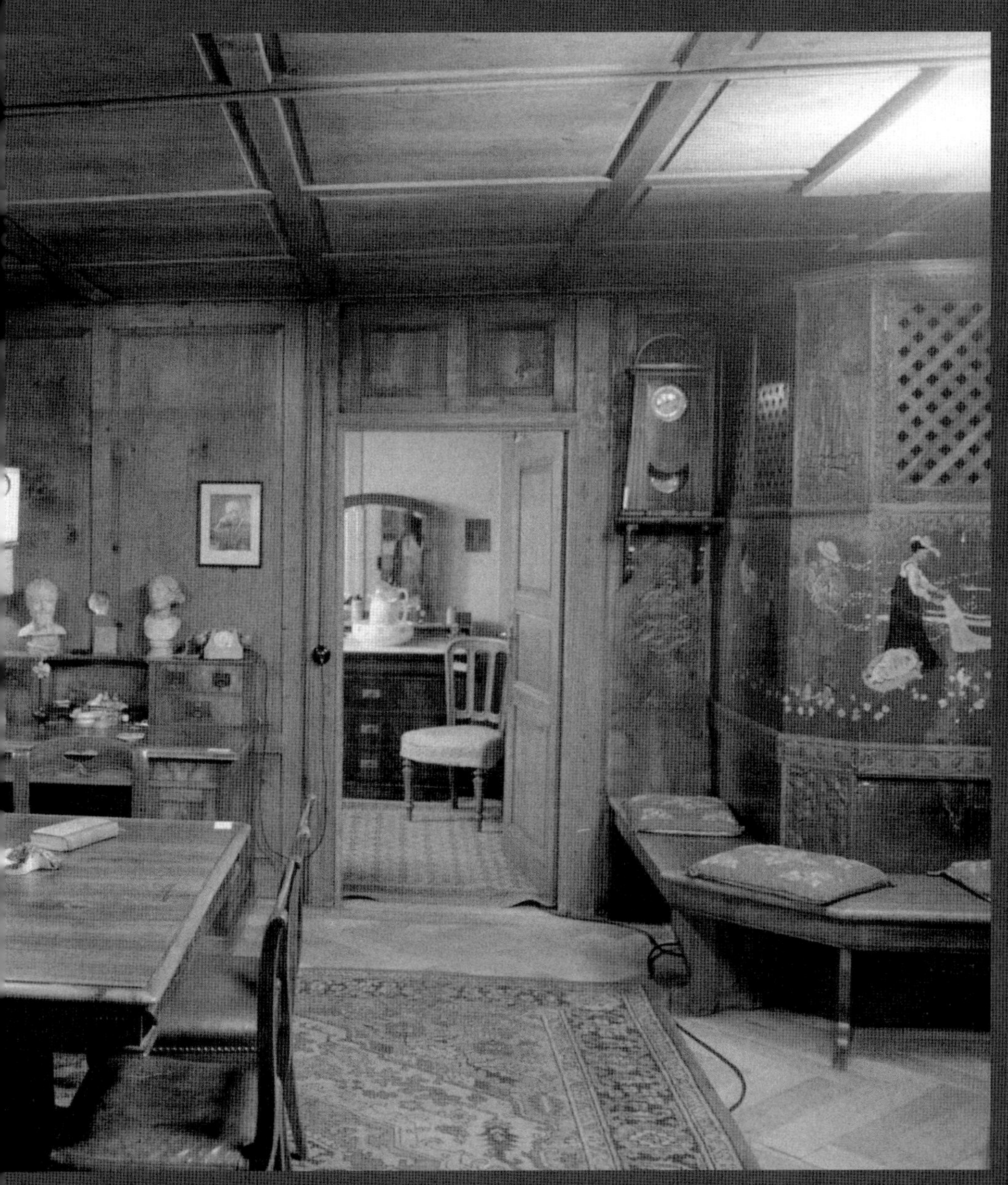

yard space, with which he was familiar. I picked him up from the railway station. His luggage consisted entirely of a mid-sized suitcase. I asked him if we had to collect the sculpture from customs. He said no: the sculpture was in his suitcase. He then took out a very small figure and, to our amazement, placed it on the pedestal that we had prepared for him. He had previously occupied himself with questions regarding monumentality and proportions. He explained to us that his sculpture's impact would be just as good from a distance of ten meters as it would be from twenty, and that this impact would be dependent on the surroundings. Although we shared his thoughts, we also thought about the workers who prepared the pedestal according to his specifications and that it would be impossible for us to advocate his concept to our client. This was not a museum or art gallery, but exhibition grounds that did not seem suitable for devotion to such experiments; even less so because Alberto . . . each time pulled out an even smaller [sculpture]."[9] But Alberto wrote in a letter at that time that he tried installing it after working for two days on the pedestal and the figure—it was probably a head—to test its impact, and that it was a good experience.[10]

In the end, the solution was to exhibit one of the *Cube* sculptures (ill. page 53) from 1933, which according to Bruno was "the only abstract artwork in the whole exhibition and something that was already passé for Alberto." A head by the sculptor Cornelia Forster was exhibited on a low pedestal in a different courtyard of the building, which to all intents and purposes recalls the typical installation of Alberto's *Grande Tête (Monumental Head)* from 1960. Should one not regard Alberto's miniature figures as a reaction against the prevailing gargantuanism of sculpture of the nineteen-thirties? Not only was the 1939 Landi, the Swiss National Exhibition in Zurich, full of such works, they also dominated the 1937 Paris World's Fair. Bruno Giacometti is in any case still one of the greatest promoters of his brother's memory today.

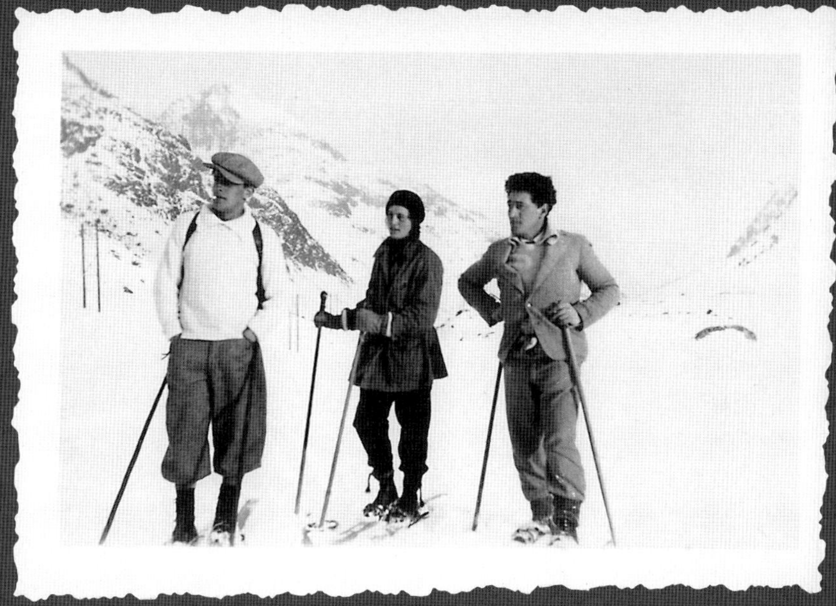

33

FATHER AND SON

"I see my father pacing back and forth at the easel and I still smell the fine aroma of the paint and feel again the warmth of the oven in winter. Nothing pleased me more than to run to the studio after school and to sit down in my corner near the window and browse through books and draw. There are things that I believe have influenced me ever since and will continue to influence me, but they are very difficult to differentiate from the rest and distinguish from each other. I feel very attached to the time when I was twelve years old, and that includes all areas; I feel myself at almost the same point and I do not know precisely what time means." Alberto Giacometti wrote this to Peter F. Althaus, the author of the essay "Zwei Generationen Giacometti" (Two Generations of Giacomettis) for the March 1958 issue of the Swiss art magazine *Du* devoted to the subject matter of "Fathers and Sons."

For a long time, in fact until well into the nineteen-seventies, Giovanni Giacometti was far better known than his son Alberto. The crises of modern mankind reflected in his son's works do not seem to be his principal subject matter. His pictures convey at first sight a very special harmony that is founded primarily on color. I was much more open to Giovanni's works as a child when my parents took me along on museum visits. I was enthusiastic about the 1912 portrait of his daughter Ottilia I saw and fell eternally in love with at the Oskar Reinhart Foundation in Winterthur.

Giovanni Giacometti is one of Switzerland's most under-valued early modernist artists. He undeservedly stands in the shadow of his friends Ferdinand Hodler (1853–1918), Segantini, and Amiet. But it is the breaks in his works that make them complicated upon closer examination; his indecisiveness, his seemingly never-ending efforts to suitably harmonize light and color within a pictorial composition,

34

make him an exemplary model of the twentieth-century artist who could not or would not take the final step in the direction of abstraction.

But Giovanni had a very realistic estimation of himself and his place in the history of art. In a letter dated May 3, 1927, addressed to his sons in Paris he wrote: "It was my dream to conquer Paris, but now you are the ones who will conquer it, with sculpture, with industry [by which he likely meant "crafts"], and with architecture."[11] Giovanni not only assigned roles to his sons here—sculpture to Alberto, craft to Diego, and architecture to Bruno—he also disclosed that he probably would never be able to fulfill the demands he placed on himself and that he would never really break through as an artist. But his sons were to fulfill his dream, particularly one of them: Alberto. He was even more explicit in a letter to Daniel Baud-Bovy dated August 26, 1917: "By nature more contemplative than combative, I have unfortunately ensconced myself in my mountains, quite alone and isolated."[12]

In this letter he candidly addressed the crucial influences that other painters had on his art; he mentions "Segantinism," Pointillism, and the model of Hodler. From the very beginning, it was his "vision of light" (in his words, "vision lumineuse") that had endured, a "childhood dream" he had constantly attempted to realize.

But was the father, who made a name for himself as a painter of color and light prior to the First World War and then increasingly grew less expressive, still exemplary for the son despite his (supposed) failure? The attempt was not only everything for Alberto; he could also claim that the more you failed, the more you succeeded—as he expressed in a 1965 film portrait by Ernst Scheidegger and Peter Münger. Alberto's text on André Derain published in 1957 in the magazine *Derrière le Miroir* contains passages that could equally apply to his father. Derain was unable to follow up his success prior to the First World War as a Fauvist; he was "at a place that continually demanded too much of him, he was afraid of the impossible, and every work was already a failure before he began it. None of the foundations, none of the certainties . . . had meaning for him any more. . . . Yet perhaps he only wanted to capture a little of the appearance of things, the wonderful, attractive, and unknown appearance of everything around him."[13]

Giovanni Giacometti
was his son's first and probably
most important teacher.

Giovanni laid the foundations for Alberto's career. An innkeeper's son from the remote Val Bregaglia, he was the first member of his family to take the astonishing and certainly not universally accepted step of becoming an artist. As an artist's son, it was surely much easier and perhaps even "normal" for Alberto to follow in his father's footsteps, and he did not have to convince anyone in his family.

It seems possible to perceive the differences in self-awareness that characterized father and son when comparing their self-portraits. The father's self-portraits almost exclusively show an artist seeking self-assurance, who questions himself. The 1921 self-portrait by his approximately 20-year-old son (ill. page 49) is completely different. Half kneeling, half sitting, Alberto exudes so much self-confidence that the frame can barely contain him. Is he still sitting on the chair, or has he shifted his weight entirely to his left knee? His pose may also result from the fact that he has positioned himself as best he could to paint his reflection in the distant mirror (he was right-handed, but appears here left-handed).

The ambiguity of this pose, which lends the painting exceptional dynamism, might also have been influenced by the paintings of Ferdinand Hodler, the godfather of Alberto's brother Bruno, with whose art the Giacometti household was very familiar. Hodler deliberately employed improbable poses as a stylistic means to lend vitality to his pictures; one only has to recall his famous *Woodcutter*, whose pose, while conveying amazing force, will by no means permit him to cut down the tree. Kneeling figures such as the one in Alberto's self-portrait can also be found in the art of classical antiquity, for example the statue of Heracles from the east pediment of the Temple of Aphaia on the Greek island of Aegina. And as Christian Klemm recently observed, Alberto, a great admirer of Egyptian art, stylized his head in accordance with the appearance of the pharaoh Akhenaten.[14]

Alberto very blithely made eclectic use of art history's storehouse and created something uniquely his own in the process. Without wanting to negate the still visible awkwardness in the composition and his approach to the body, the young artist nevertheless succeeded in creating a work that can be mentioned in the same breath with other, more famous artist self-portraits, especially the one in the Louvre painted by Nicolas Poussin in 1649–50, with which Alberto was probably familiar through a reproduction. The fact that in comparison with Poussin's picture, Alberto's self-portrait is reversed from left to right does not mean that he did not model his own self-portrait after it. The composition and the distribution of the zones of color resemble the construction of the great French painter's

36

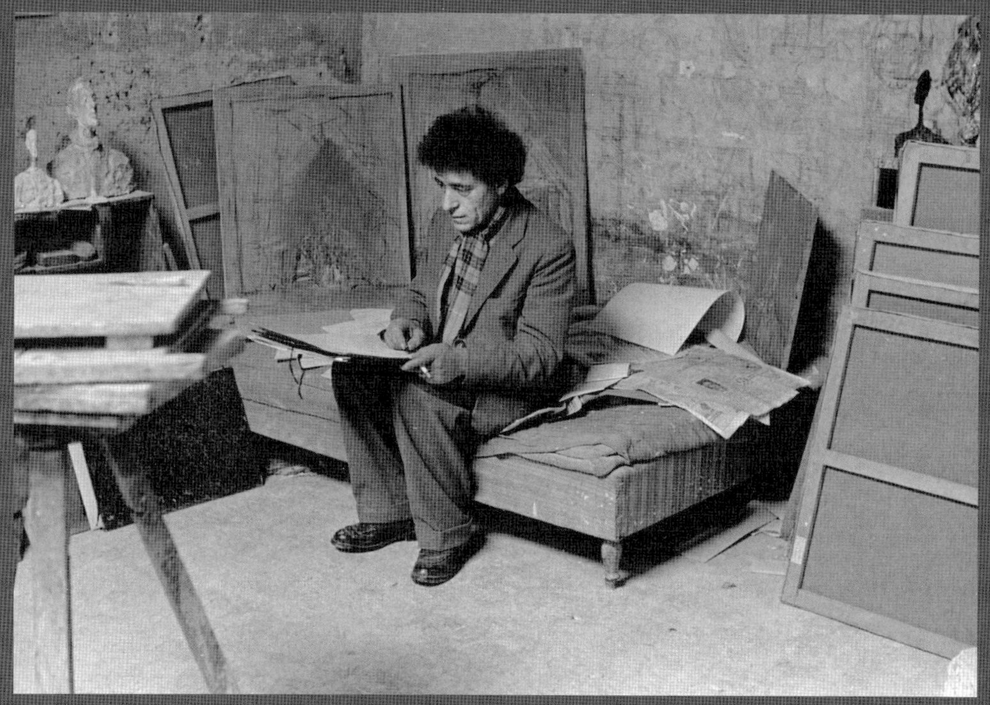

Drawing in the Parisian studio,
ca. 1953

picture. The position of the head, the gaze that is half cast in shadows, the placement of the arms, and especially the truncated rectangles in the background possibly suggesting other, as yet unpainted pictures—whereby the head of Poussin's muse on the left of his picture recurs in Giacometti's portrait on the right as a form of the wheel of a printing press—all indicate a paraphrase of one of art history's most famous artist self-portraits. Alberto's glance is not the same self-questioning glance from his father's self-portrait; one can already recognize here the uncompromising explorer of reality we are familiar with from Ernst Scheidegger's photographs and films (ill. pages 37, 80/81).

Although the young Alberto may have been more carefree than his father, he was still deeply influenced by Giovanni in the early nineteen-twenties, especially as regards his palette and technique. In fact, some visitors even thought that Alberto's paintings hanging in his father's studio were made by Giovanni himself.[15] Giovanni Giacometti was his son's first and probably most important teacher. While it might seem somewhat melodramatic to characterize Alberto as his father's artistic heir, it is nevertheless true. Great hopes were placed in this son ever since his birth and the enthusiastic father even celebrated his newborn son virtually as a savior, as a blessed child.

The fact that Alberto indeed developed the talent expected of him must have overjoyed his father. Alberto was encouraged accordingly, and he evidently soon began to play a special role in the family. As Bruno once recalled: "... our parents encouraged his [Alberto's] habit of incessantly drawing, painting, modeling, and so it was a matter of course for everybody in our house to be drawn or painted."[16] This is an important point—it was entirely "normal" to be an artist in the Giacometti household and a highly gifted child like Alberto was surely able to pursue his passion as if it were the most ordinary thing in the world. And his parents granted him the time to do so, even permitting Alberto to break off his regular schooling to devote himself to art. In May 1919, Giovanni wrote to Cuno Amiet that he and his son were working side by side, enabling him to "observe his talents and development close up."[17]

Nothing was safe
from Alberto.

What were the father's lessons like? For a start, Alberto surely did everything his father did as an artist: every family member sat for Giovanni, and soon they also sat for Alberto as well. Nothing was safe from Alberto. All those present were "mesmerized by his obsession to

38

present his way of seeing to the others," Bruno Giacometti recalled. "I drew in order to let myself go, in order to cope. The pencil was my weapon," said Alberto in a 1963 conversation with Jean Clay.[18] Drawing, modeling, and painting seem to have been his playthings.

Modeling was practiced with Plasticine, the material of which Alberto's first heads were made. Giovanni himself took part and also modeled. Bruno recalled: "Alberto modeled his first sculpture after my brother Diego in 1914. He used Plasticine, not clay. It was not the colored Plasticine that children use, but earth-colored; my father bought a kilo of it and also made a few figures from it. In 1915, Alberto modeled my head; it was a very stylized head with curly hair."[19] Incidentally, already at that time Alberto complained about his sitters to his godfather Cuno Amiet: "I modeled the heads of Diego and Bruno, and they were very fidgety models."[20] For the rest of his life, he demanded that his sitters be absolutely stationary.

It is safe to say that the father encouraged his son to copy the works of the old and modern masters from reproductions. His parents' library contained ample material of this kind. He saw himself "in Stampa, at the window, around 1914, while concentrating on copying a Japanese woodcut—I could still describe every detail of it," Alberto wrote in his 1965 "Notes sur les copies."[21] Knowledge of art history was extraordinarily important for his father. Even later, when Alberto was in Paris, his father continued to give him advice in this regard, for example in a letter dated February 1, 1922: "You cannot look at the masters of the past often enough, and you must do so whenever you have the opportunity. New palaces can only be built on strong foundations, and the study of the great old and modern masters (but especially the old ones, because the others learnt from them) should run in parallel with the study of nature."[22] Alberto would heed these paternal words for the rest of his life.

But there is also an indication of the nature of Giovanni's practical training; it can be found in one of Alberto's poetic letters to his friend Lucas Lichtenhan. The seventeen-year-old described in it how he sat in his father's studio painting an illustration for the fairy tale "Snow White": "The sky was so hard to do, it was dark blue and you had to leave all the stars white. It was hard work and resulted in really big irregular stars."[23] "You had to leave all the stars white": there is no better way to learn how to see and draw contours. Such exercises still form the foundation of every drawing book today. They serve to train the ability to perceive foreground and background as abstract planes which, when seen simultaneously, create the illusion of bodies in space without defining them by means of outlines. An

39

examination of Giovanni Giacometti's works gives one the impression that handling contrasting color surfaces was one of the central problems with which he grappled. But Alberto's childhood drawings are conceived to large extent on the basis of the outlines; he still had to learn to how to develop objects less in terms of their outlines and more from a center, as he would later do. It is not surprising that he could precisely recall all of that in his letter to his friend.

Alberto's way
of perceiving nature
was much more egocentric,
but also much more
precise than his father's.

For Giovanni, the capturing of reality was decisive, and indeed not merely the external appearances of things, but their essence. The Zurich painter Adolf Mohler, who was a student of Giovanni Giacometti's for a time in the early nineteen-twenties, once reported how his teacher repeatedly emphasized that it was "not one's own thoughts based on mere human rationality, but seeing, as an assimilation of nature's greatness, the sensation of and being fulfilled by what one sees—that is what makes an artist."[24]

In this respect, too, Alberto followed his father's advice for the rest of his life. There were, however, clear differences between his approach and his father's, and these already became evident while he was still learning. The artist's task was to express his admiration for the grandeur of creation—that was Giovanni's motivation. Alberto's way of perceiving nature was much more egocentric, but also much more precise than his father's. Because one can only experience reality for himself, it could, technically speaking, only be depicted in relation to one's self. Every step that goes beyond this subjectivity, that attempts to depict a universal reality, is infinitely more difficult. The causes of Giacometti's often invoked crises, all of which revolved around issues of regarding the appropriation of reality, may well be found here. If one wants to describe Giacometti's manner of appropriating reality, one would have to add the representation of *appearance* to capturing outer reality and the essence, in the sense of the word "vision" that means not only "sight," but also inner "seeing" and with it "appearance."

One can see from his attempts to fashion his father's head around 1927 how the young Alberto approached the personality of his admired and beloved role model without, however, deciding

40

on a single "valid" image. Alberto not only painted portraits of his father's head, but also produced a portrait in the round, as well as a kind of scored relief portrait, in addition to a marble version in which Giovanni's features are only suggested, yet appear extremely animated when seen in oblique light. And then there is also a mask-like version of his father that Véronique Wiesinger once characterized as a type of fetish. It can be seen in some of Ernst Scheidegger's photographs that capture a particular studio situation; it is especially conspicuous in the photograph of *Femme au chariot* (ill. page 78). Did Alberto really wish to be continually reminded of his father in this way?

The anecdote about Alberto having painted over the portrait head of his father by Auguste de Niederhäusern because he could not bear it unless it was colored is particularly revealing in this context. Although his father was said to have been astonished, he did not reproach Alberto. But Giovanni did not always show such understanding for his gifted son: "Once, when I was about eighteen or nineteen, I was in [my father's] studio drawing some pears that were on a table, at the normal distance of a still life. And the pears kept getting tiny. I'd begin again, and they'd always go back to exactly the same size. My father got irritated and said: 'But just do them as they are, as you see them.' And he corrected them. I tried to do them as he wanted but I couldn't stop myself rubbing out. I kept on rubbing out, and half an hour later they were exactly the same size to the millimeter as the first ones."[25]

The problem of depicting objects in relation to himself as an observer, and the object in the distance that separated him from it, would become relevant again much later when Alberto returned to working from models in the nineteen-thirties. Giovanni must have been familiar with the same difficulties his son was having. He himself had dealt often enough with the representation of distance and size relationships. A good example is his painting *Sunny Hillside with Goats and Sheep* (ca. 1900), which reflects the extent to which the Alps, especially in Val Bregaglia, confronted artists with the problem of estimating size. As was mentioned above, nowhere else but in the high mountains do small things appear large and large things small.

Their father's death on June 25, 1933, was a terrible blow for the family, especially for Alberto. He spent that summer in Stampa, arranging Giovanni's estate. Among other things, Alberto kept a selection of his father's paintings. In 1934, the gravestone he made was placed in the cemetery at Borgonovo, where he himself would be laid to rest after his own death on January 11, 1966. Alberto always remained extremely grateful to his father, repeatedly emphasizing the liberties he had been permitted. In a note from 1934, written shortly after his father's death, Alberto recalled, "Everything went as it had to go, Father was happy about my success and knew that I loved his pictures, and what a great, great admiration I had for him."[26]

Alberto Giacometti not only had the capacity to convey his sensory perceptions as a draughtsman, sculptor, and painter, but also extremely intensely in written form. And he could do this in numerous languages as well: in Italian, French, German, and naturally also in his own Val Bregaglia dialect, which derives from Italian. He seems to have strongly relived his own reading and visual experiences. On the way to Stampa he once had a vision of encountering the "apothecary from Chamounix," from Gottfried Keller's eponymous narrative poem, who had just "gunned down his woman"; he watched him for a long time, as he wrote to Lucas Lichtenhan on April 8, 1918.

These facilities might also be related to a sense of abandon that gradually decreased with age, the feeling of looming failure because everything was only an "attempt" anyway. Whoever can do anything, or almost anything, is probably the first to discern the discrepancy between the result and the perfection he had intended in his own work. For Giacometti, it almost seemed easier to depict this intended perfection in writing. This also made him interesting for the group of the Surrealists headed by the poet André Breton, and one could claim that Alberto's literary contributions to Surrealism are almost as significant as his so-called Surrealist artworks, which he incidentally saw rather as a further means of depicting reality.

A quote from one of the letters written to his friend Lucas Lichtenhan in June 1918 illustrates Giacometti's magniloquence. He was sixteen years old at the time and was writing about a school excursion. The orthographic mistakes in the original letter show that German was not his mother tongue, but the letter also reveals how intensely he must have occupied himself with German literature, particularly Classicism and Romanticism. Friedrich von Schiller (perhaps his poem *Der Spaziergang [The Walk]*) and Joseph von Eichendorff do not seem far removed. One should pay particular attention to the change of perspective from the view off into the distance to the view to the microcosm:

"I passed through large meadows. Straight ahead of me, the forests and the Alps alternated like waves, but to the rear a chain of wonderful mountains could be seen. These mountains, full of the finest and most beautiful colors, were enveloped in a kind of glowing, silky fog, and the lights and shadows of the most distant snowcapped mountains melted together with the lights and shadows of rosy, bluish, and multiform clouds. But shadows of these clouds played with the mountains and the valley. They slid and moved—always changing their shapes—across the fields and villages from the Rhine Valley and over heaps and rocks irrespective of form, and so they changed constantly. And the mountains shone once in the most wonderful colors, only to draw back shortly thereafter into a very distant deep violet; at the same a golden peak emerged from the blue mass. The Rhine Valley lay in a deep, calm green. All of this was large and sublime; but if you directed your eye at the ground, it was attracted to the finest of beauties. Flowers lay there transfigured by the thousands. I had to sit down again at every new flower and observe it. After a moment, the flowers became increasingly rarefied; each leaf was given new life, every small part of it had a different, unmentionably beautiful color. Every flower was as large, as beautiful as a whole world, and each one differed from the other. Every blue, every yellow flower revealed an abundance of shapes and colors that caused astonishment and amazement. There were heaps that, with the many flowers, with the dainty greenish hues, showed a wondrous beauty. Large luminous bees and crimson creatures and thousands of others sat exquisitely on the calyxes. I finally began to hurry in order not to remain too far behind. It was as if I moved through an enchanted land; there was something new, something fine wherever one looked. A constant chime of bells rang in my ears, and when the pealing gradually died down, birds, which I could not see, began to sing and screech. A herd of goats gathered between the gray stones and then the wind began to blow, and it whistled and howled. Large clouds moved wildly about the proud, high masses of rocks. When I looked at the small beautiful things of the ground and then the wild big picture out there, I shuddered at the thought that the enormity of beauty comprises an infinite number of small, fine, and dainty beauties, and nature seemed even more sublime! But now we are here, and it is so cozy and pleasant. I would like to write much, much more to you, dear Lux, but as you can see, the paper is full; I will write you a longer letter soon. As always, your Tsching!"

"Tsching," his nickname, means "the Italian" in the Swiss vernacular and is often used derogatorily. The abrupt conclusion of the text was a stylistic device that Giacometti often made use of later. It suggests that what had been written was only a small detail from an immeasurably large whole that could be continued at will, similar to the notion of seeing his artistic production as a kind of never-ending process that, when abruptly interrupted, produces a completed work, as it were.

In his childhood recollections entitled "Hier, sables mouvants" (Yesterday, Shifting Sands) published in 1933 in the magazine *Le Surréalisme au service de la Révolution,* Giacometti wrote that as a child he was thoroughly selective in regards to the events that streamed in on him: "As a child (between four and seven years), what I saw of the outside world was only things of a kind that could give me pleasure. These were above all stones and trees, and rarely more than one object at a time."[27] These introductory remarks are followed by the description of a monolith lying near his house, the inside of which contained a cavity into which the children liked to repair. His father—who else?—pointed it out to him. The intense experience of contained volume that this boulder seems to have triggered in Alberto is juxtaposed in the text to a pointy pyramid-like stone that he considered particularly threatening. The two stones can surely be interpreted as an encounter between the female and male principles, similar to the 1928–29 sculpture *Homme et femme (Man and Woman)* (ill. page 50). Here it is most important to point to the playfully experienced significance of the boulders as space-defining elements—as vessels on the one hand, and as objects in space on the other—as well as the emotions they trigger. The text then describes further notions regarding the feeling of security that contrast with inhospitality and frostiness. The descriptions conclude with shocking and sadistic obsessions in a gruesome fairy-tale world:

"As far as recurring obsessive thoughts of this kind are concerned, I recall months on end during which I could not fall asleep unless I had previously fantasized about crossing a dense forest at sundown and reaching a gray castle located at a hidden and completely unknown place. There I killed two men who could not defend themselves against me, one of whom was about seventeen years old and always seemed quite pale and scared, while the other wore a suit of armor on which something shone like gold on the left side. I raped the two women after first ripping off their clothes: a woman aged

45

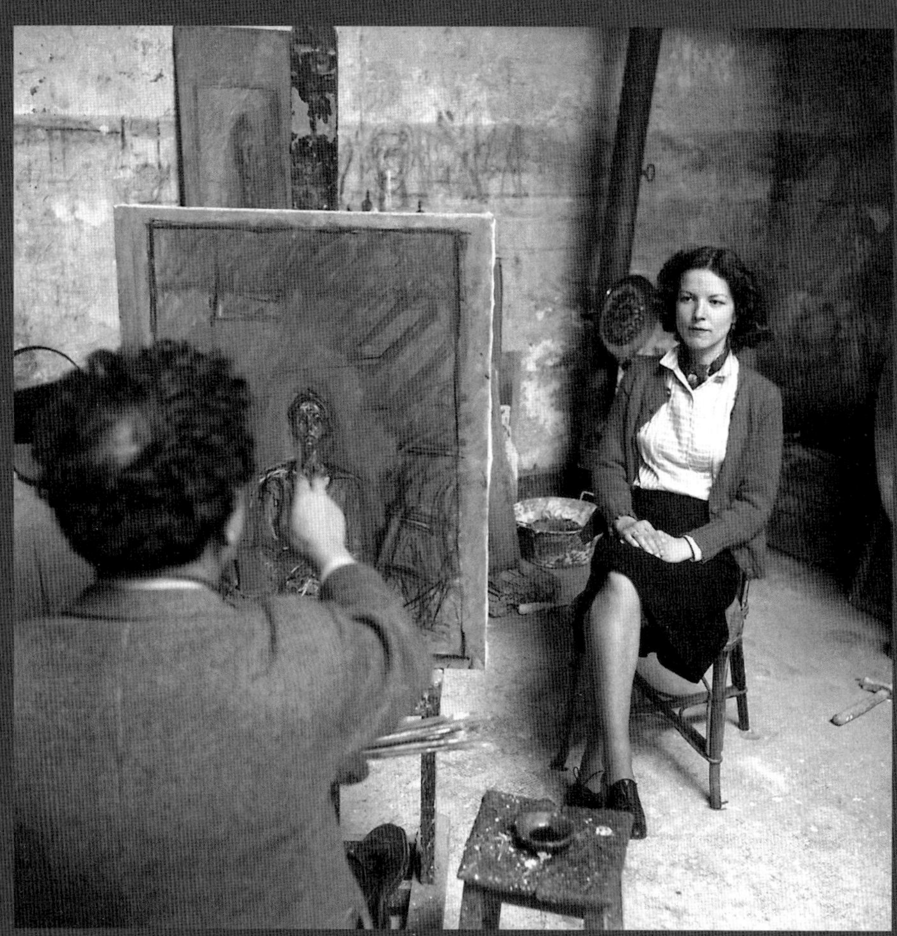

Annette sits for Alberto, 1954

about 32, dressed entirely in black and with a face the color of alabaster, and her daughter about whom white veils wafted. Their screams and laments echoed across the forest. I killed them too, but very slowly (it was now nighttime), often next to a pond with moldy green water in front of the castle. Each time somewhat differently. Afterwards I burned down the castle and fell peacefully asleep."

To what extent this text represents an exaggerated stylization of violent adolescent fantasies formulated with a view to a certain shock effect is anyone's guess. In any case, Giacometti's gruesome, even sadistic works such as *Femme égorgée (Woman with Her Throat Cut)* from 1933, for example, come to mind. The text also casts light on his relationship to women, which was by no means unproblematic. As he openly confessed to Jean Clay in 1963, he considered himself "très déficient sexuellement," i.e., sexually very inadequate, which, however, might be related to his supposed impotence.[28] The idea of love as a suspicious and sticky mixture of emotions and body movements always embarrassed him, Giacometti said. This might also be the reason why he preferred attachments to prostitutes over love relationships. And if he was interested in women who were not prostitutes, then they were women who seem to have been very unconventional, and not only in sexual terms.

The women with whom Alberto had more involved romantic attachments were always his models, and they were also crucial for his artistic development. Isabel Nicholas (1912–1992), for example, who later married journalist Sefton Delmer and composer Alan Rawsthorne and who was romantically linked with Alberto in the nineteen-thirties and again shortly after his return to Paris in 1945, was the model who enabled his return to figuration. She later also sat for Francis Bacon and introduced Giacometti to him. In 1943, Alberto met the then twenty-year-old Annette Arm (1923–1993) and the two of them married in 1949. Annette not only had a youthful and carefree charm, but she also liked, as Simone de Beauvoir tellingly wrote, a certain amount of violence which, in the face of her husband's preferences, must have also been coupled with the willingness to make sacrifices. It is said that she had an affair with Alberto's favorite model of the late-nineteen fifties, the Japanese philosophy professor Isaku Yanaihara. She was Alberto's most important model of the postwar period and probably the only one who posed nude for him at that time. Some years before his death, Alberto additionally made the acquaintance of a young woman, born in 1938, who introduced herself to him in 1958 as "Caroline" at the Bar Chez Adrien. He admired her love of risk taking and her lack of morals; with the assistance of her entourage,

47

she bled him completely dry. He not only paid her lawyer when she once went to prison, he also bought her a convertible sports car and an apartment. But she "rewarded" him, however, with her services as a model. The approximately thirty portraits Giacometti made of her are among the best and most striking works of his final years (ill. page 57). The history of art owes the suite of lithographs entitled *Paris sans fin (Paris Without End)* to the joyrides they undertook together in the convertible, during which he sketched. While it would certainly be an exaggeration to suggest that Giacometti subliminated sexuality by means of artistic activities, his relationships to his models could also be exceedingly intimate without being physical. At least his stare was possessive; this has been reported by all those who ever sat for him.

In his brief essay on Jacques Callot (1592–1635) and Callot's gruesome pictures that were published in 1945 in the magazine *Labyrinthe*, Giacometti characterized the sadistic egocentrism depicted in "Hier, sables mouvants" as being typical of artists.[29] One must read this text together with his childhood recollections. Both provide a fascinating, but nevertheless problematic literary self-portrait: the artist—one can perhaps also say the highly gifted person—who acts in his thoughts from the security and stronghold of his own ego without consideration or moral standards.

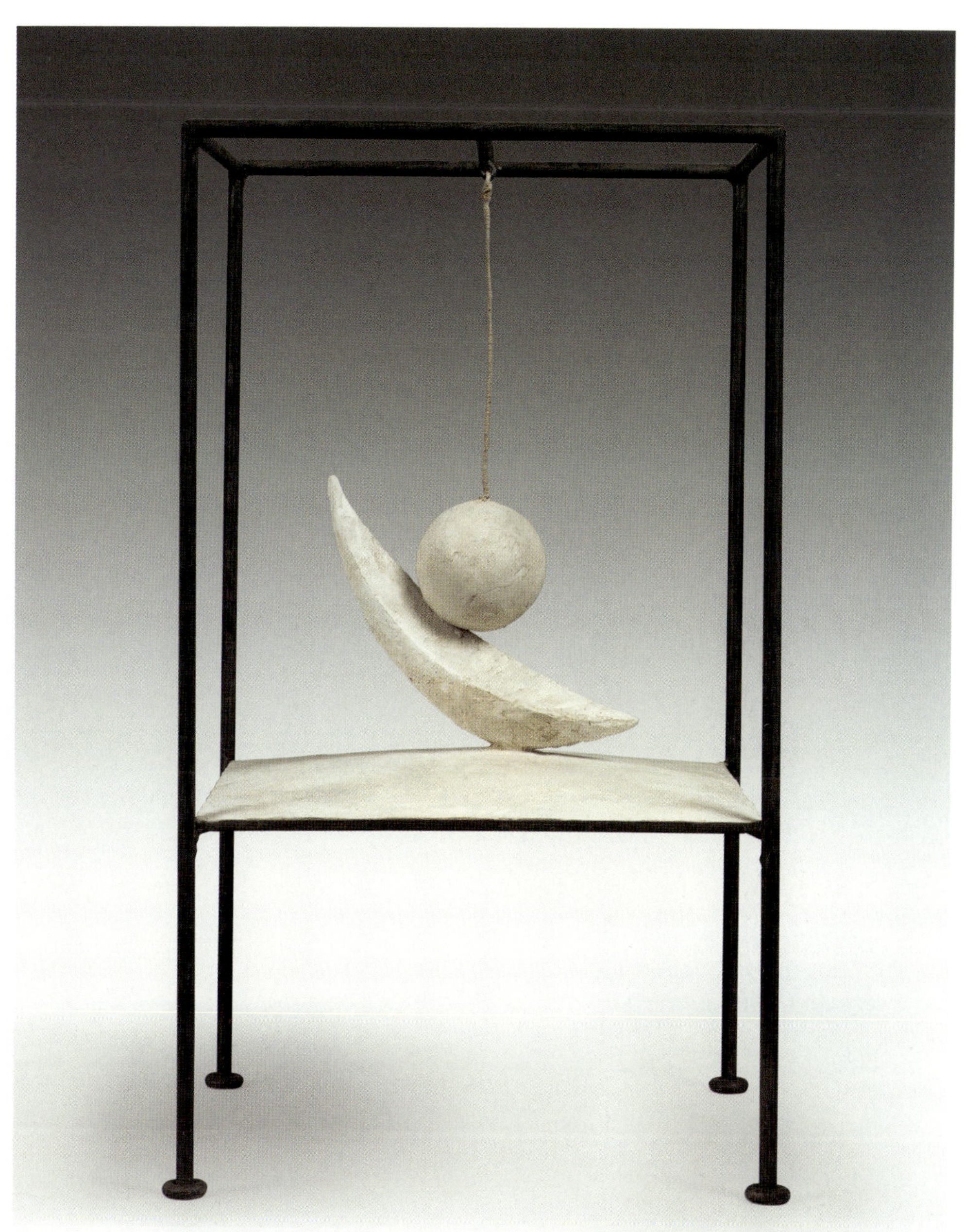

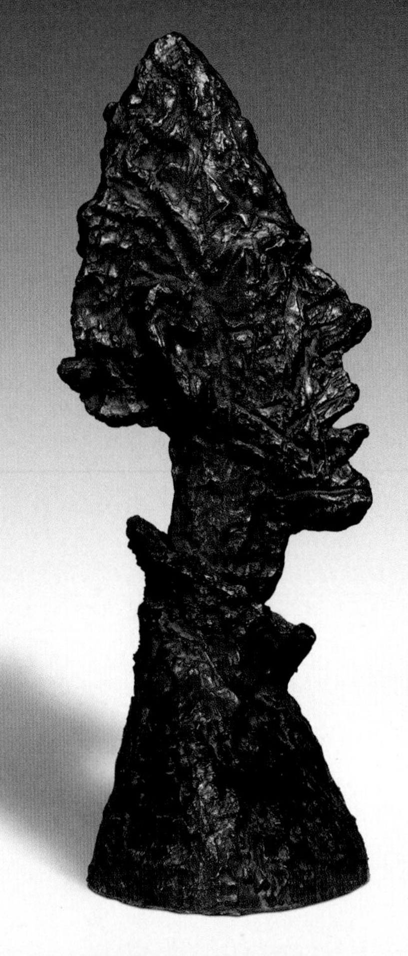

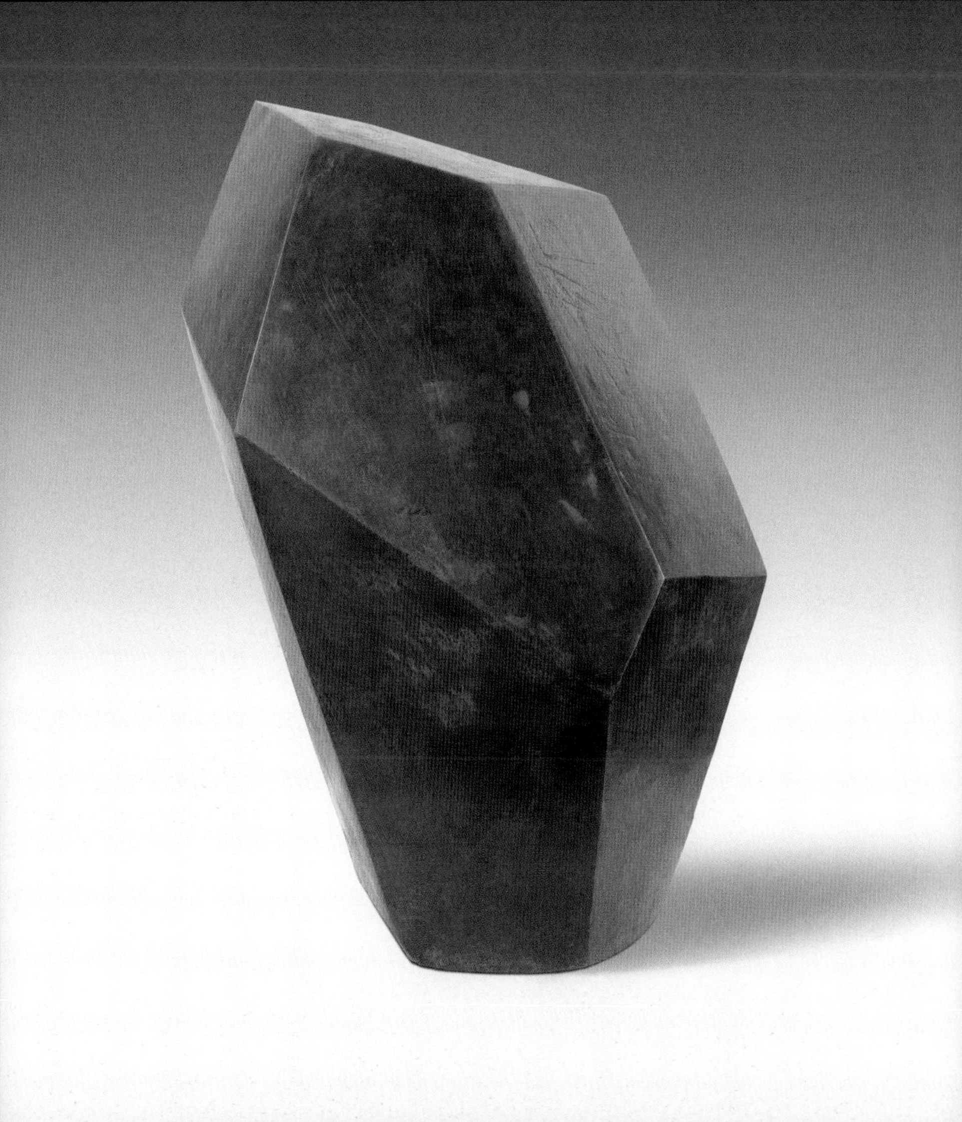

LE CHARIOT (THE CHARIOT) 1950
Bronze on pedestal, 167 x 69 x 69 cm
Alberto Giacometti Foundation, Zurich

L'HOMME QUI MARCHE SOUS LA PLUIE
(MAN WALKING IN THE RAIN) 1948
Bronze, pained, 47 x 77.6 x 15.9 cm
Fondation Beyeler, Riehen / Basel

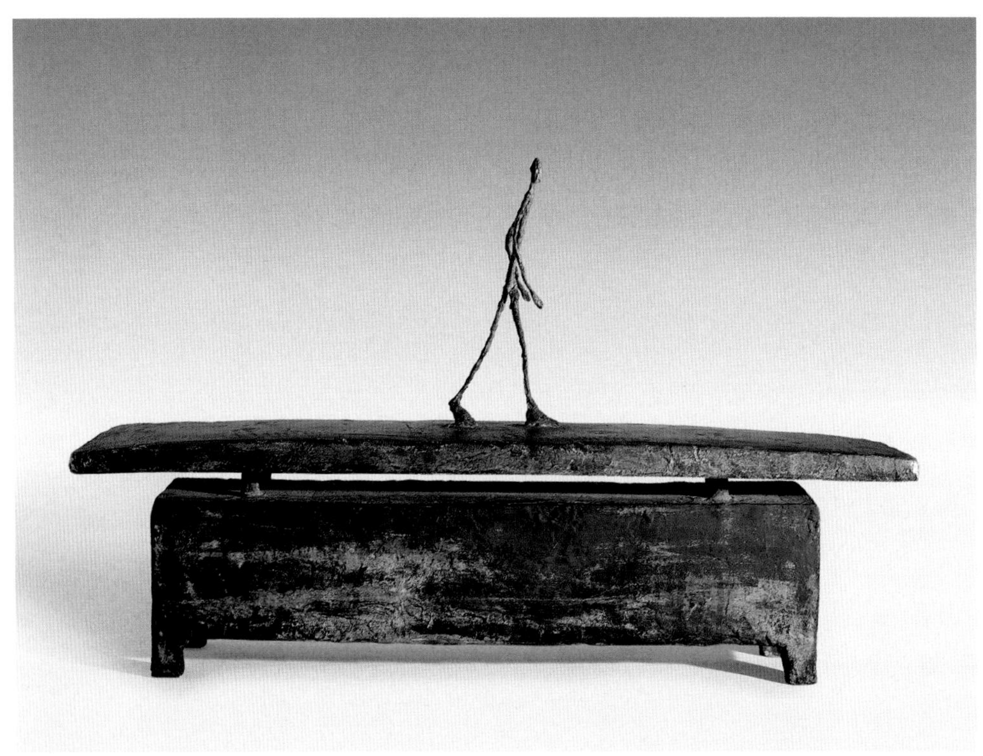

54

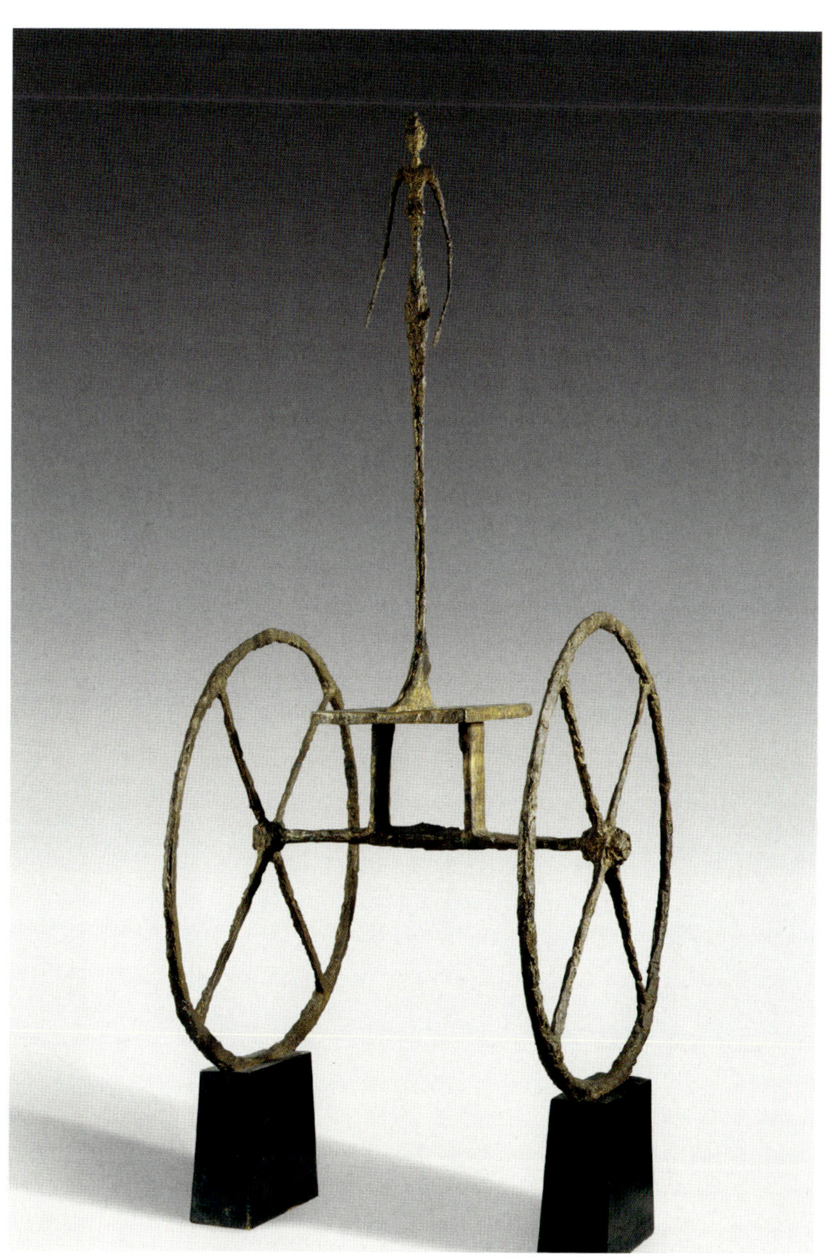

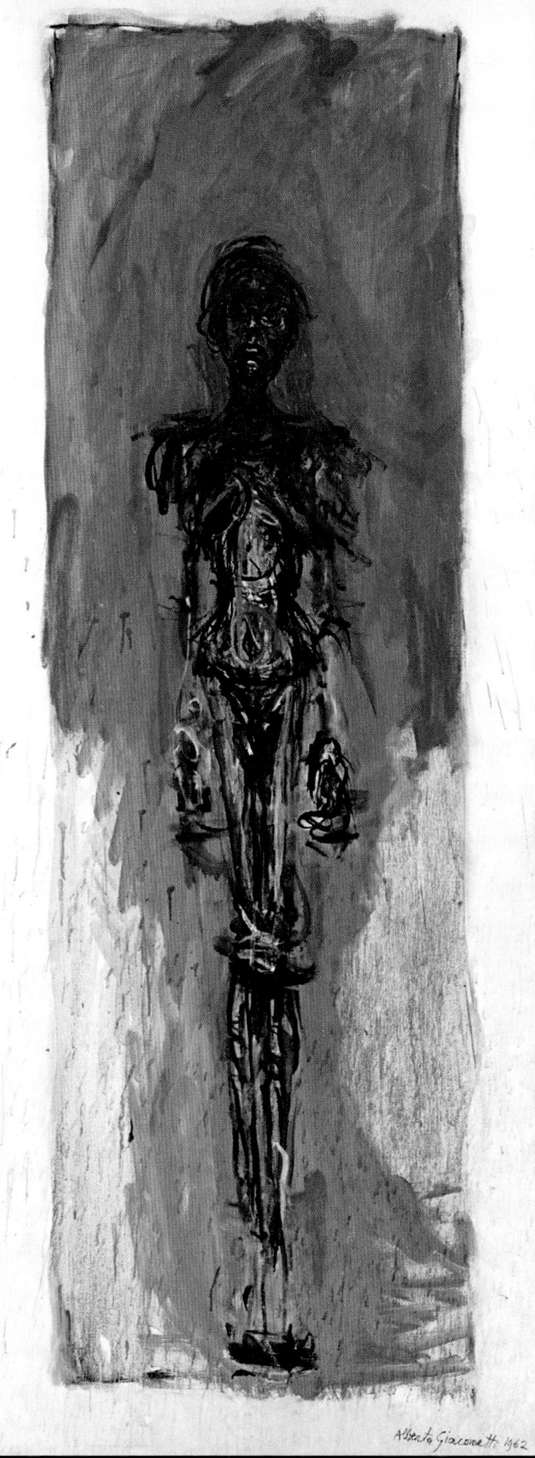

Alberto Giacometti 1962

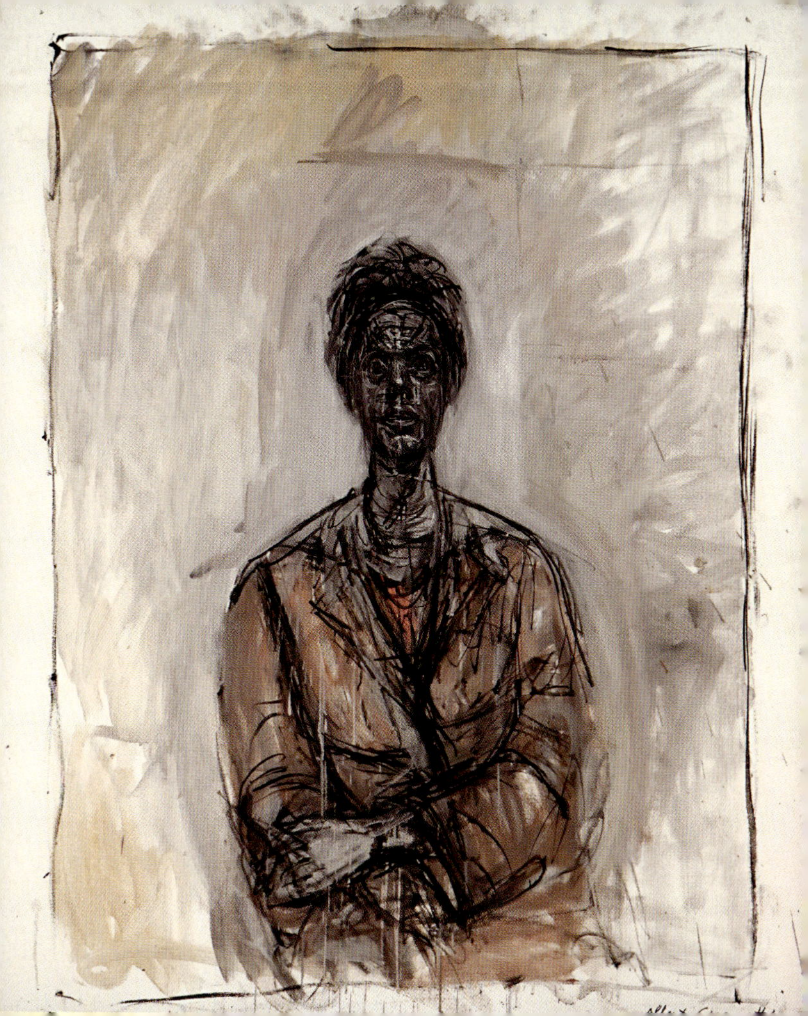

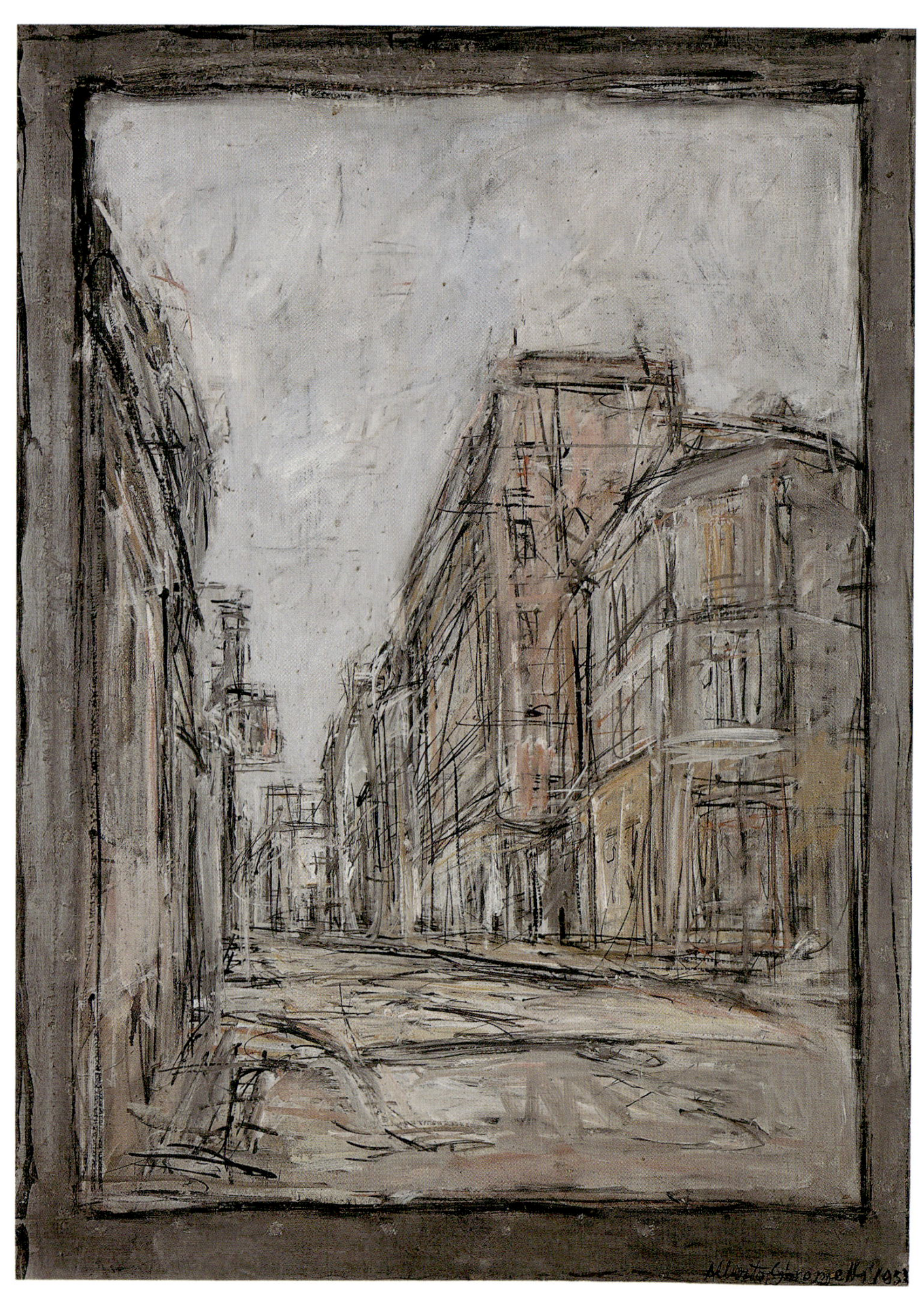

LA RUE (THE STREET
IN FRONT OF THE STUDIO) 1952
Oil on canvas, 73 x 54 cm
Fondation Beyeler, Riehen / Basel

58

GAMES, EMOTIONS,
AND SPACE:
THE STUDIO

As he wrote in 1947 in a letter to his New York art deal-er Pierre Matisse, the younger son of Henri Matisse, Giacometti was concerned in the nineteen-twenties and early thirties with representing his inner emotions, which drew the attention of the Surrealists: "I was no longer inter-ested in the outer shape of beings but in the emotions I felt in my own life."[30] The reason he provided was the creative crisis that, accord-ing to the autobiographical notes in Jacques Dupin's 1962 monograph, manifested itself in the fact that he was now unable to model or to paint what he saw, as he had done so well in the past. This problem had smoldered for a long while and had already begun even before his time as a student in Antoine Bourdelle's class at the Académie de la Grande Chaumière in Paris, which he attended from 1922 to 1926. He was thus unable to produce a satisfying sculptural form for the head of his cousin Bianca, in whom he had unhappily fallen in love, while in Rome in 1921. He was no longer able to work from a model, from nature, as he previously could, and in his "despair" began to cre-ate objects "from memory," which, as he also wrote to Pierre Matisse, represented "a certain part of my vision of reality." One of these ob-jects is "une tête," as he called it in his letter. The piece from 1929 is now known under the title *Tête qui regarde (Gazing Head)*. It is one of the so-called "disc sculptures," which were influenced by ancient Cycladic art and were the first of Giacometti's works that really made him well known as an artist, even though he was—as always—com-pletely dissatisfied with them.

In retrospect, Alberto explained his situation from that time in a 1951 interview: "I attempted to realize in my studio from memory what I had felt in front of the model in Bourdelle's class. What I really felt was restricted to a disc that stood at a certain angle

59

in space on which there were only two indentations, if you like: the experience of verticality and horizontality that one has in front of every figure. . . . I thus began to analyze a figure: the legs, the head, the arms—and everything seemed wrong to me. I did not believe in it. I had to forgo more and more in order to approach my notion even closer, to restrict myself—omit the head, the arms, and everything. And so only a disc remained of the figure and that was never deliberate and was not satisfactory—quite the contrary. It was always disappointing that what I really had mastered as form was reduced down to so little!"[31] But what is the "certain part of my vision of reality" that this sculpture is supposed to convey? As Christian Klemm noted, *Gazing Head* is "an appearance, a thing and yet not a thing." The appearance seems incorporeal. The head gazes, but "one cannot gaze back into its eyes."[32]

As Giacometti wrote in his letter to Pierre Matisse, he subsequently built cages, or had cages built for him, that underscore incorporeality in order to lend an object as an appearance a structure and a space; he had always conceived of these cages as "transparent construction[s]" rather than "compact mass[es]." This refers to *Cage* from 1930, but particularly also to *Boule suspendue (Suspended Ball)* from 1930–31, the work that suggests the third element "in reality" that had "captivated" Giacometti alongside appearance and space: motion. The viewer was intended to truly experience this movement, and above all to have the feeling that he could set it in motion.

Giacometti's depiction of his inner emotional world by means of the elements of appearance, space, and motion demands a new form of perception on the part of the audience, an active audience. After all, it is not as if the motion of which Giacometti speaks can always be triggered by the audiences. This is in fact only possible in the case of works such as the 1932 *Main prise (Caught Hand)* in which the crank threatening the hand, and (as the title says) which causes it pain, can actually be turned (ill. page 4/5). Indeed, the objects designated as "à jeter"—to be thrown away—could theoretically be in fact thrown away, making them equally space-defining as well as potentially deadly projectiles. The ultimate kinetic object, however, is the celebrated *Boule suspendue (Suspended Ball)* of which three versions exist, one made of wood and two made of plaster (ill. page 51). Giacometti characterized them in the letter to Matisse as "a split ball suspended in a cage that can glide over a crescent moon." The Surrealists were all particularly impressed with this work, especially André Breton, who acquired the version in wood for his own collection. It "functioned" like a mind game that could be reproduced in

60

writing. The Surrealist poet René Crevel described it as follows: "One first sets in motion this wooden ball, which Giacometti fitted with a female indentation, and observes how it glides over a ledge with an elongated fruit made from the same material, but comprising a male form: both are at their wits' end, both lust after each other, and every viewer partakes in this arousal, even if one could have hardly imagined it beforehand because it ultimately involves only two smooth pieces of boxwood which, when the cord brakes the ball's momentum, cannot sink into the nirvana of satisfaction."[33]

The game
is the practice
of reality.

But even the works that were not specifically fitted with motion devices were nevertheless intended to be perceived by the viewer as movement. For example, the 1928–29 sculpture *Homme et femme (Man and Woman)* (ill. page 50): The tension of an aggressively male object is starkly contrasted with a withdrawn, spoon-like female one, whose genitals—or that which we unavoidably must identify as such— nevertheless turn towards the sharp-pointed male. It is as if two electrical generators had come together igniting a spark. The arousal triggered in this manner is reflected in the rapid upward motion of the spoon-female. Giacometti had found something here akin to a symbol for sexuality. The *Reclining Women* sculptures, particularly *Femme couchée qui rêve (Reclining Woman Who Dreams)* from the same period with its nevertheless fixed, counteracting waves, "function" in a similar manner. The 1934–35 sculpture *Mains tenant le vide (L'Objet invisible) (Hands Holding the Void [Invisible Object])* should perhaps also be comprehended as a sequence of movements: the disc that hinders the feet—or perhaps in fact falls onto them—triggers the fright or pain conveyed by the face and gesture of the hands, making this "funereal monument to his father" (Christian Klemm) a direct expression of a sense of pain. It is true of all of the works generally belonging to Giacometti's Surrealist period that they paraphrase aspects of play. Playing means practicing for reality, and this is what Giacometti, the seeker of reality, portrays here. In *On ne joue plus (No More Play)* from 1932, a metaphor for death, the game board becomes an apocalyptic cemetery where the graves give up their dead.

Play and the movement that unfolds in play require space. It is therefore hardly surprising that Giacometti had been interested in stage design since childhood, although there are only a

61

Alberto in his Parisian studio
on Rue Froidevaux, 1926
In the background, a woodcut portrait
Giovanni Giacometti's mother.
The sculpture *Tête (Head)* from 1925–26
is to the left behind him.

Alberto Giacometti before the door
of his Parisian studio on
Rue Hippolyte-Maindron, 1960

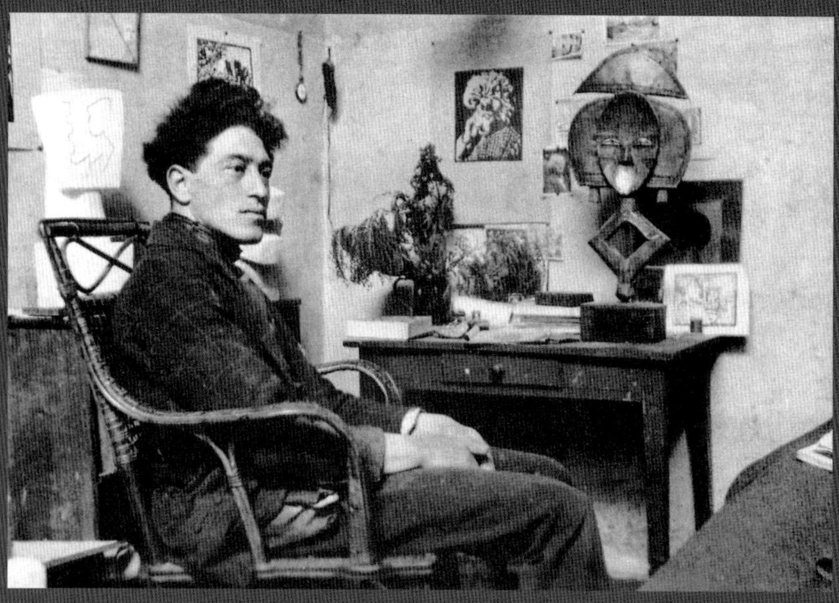

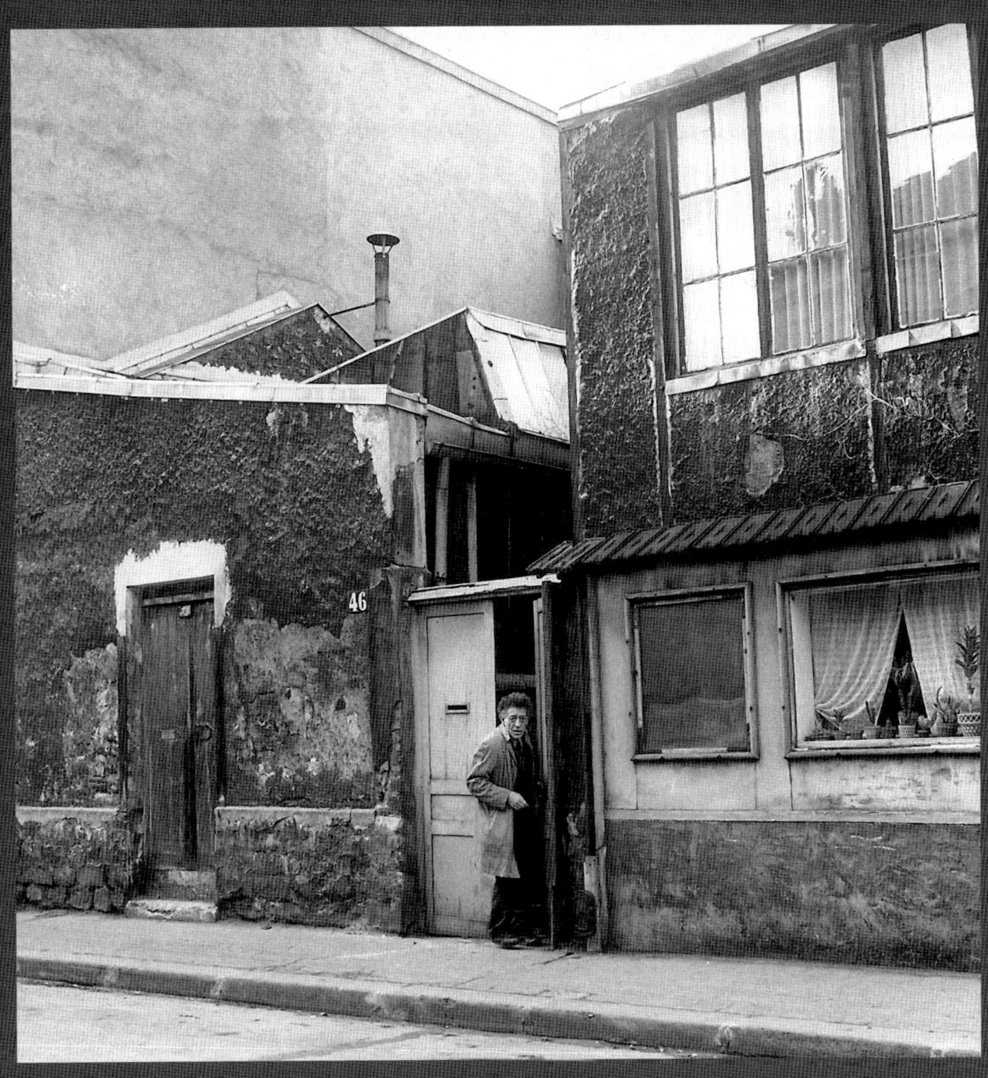
46

few designs that were in fact intended for an actual stage. The most famous is the stage design made in 1961 in collaboration with the playwright for Samuel Beckett's *Waiting for Godot* at the Théâtre de l'Odéon in Paris. The theater is the place where feelings are portrayed and made visible for an audience. It is nevertheless imposing that the stage is a real space at the same time, but one that can also make inner spaces visible.

In this context, one can also consider Giacometti's studio as theater-like staging. For him, it was a working space as well as a space for thought. From 1927 on, Giacometti rented a studio in a complex of barracks on Rue Hippolyte-Maindron 46 in Paris that he used for the rest of his life and where he also lived if he did not go to a hotel to sleep (ill. page 63). Adjacent spaces were later rented, including his brother's studio. Annette also lived there when she first came to Paris in 1947 and stayed there until Alberto bought her an apartment. The studio, which included a gallery that could be accessed via a narrow flight of stairs, could only be heated by a round iron stove; one washed at the cold water faucet in the courtyard where the toilet was also located. Electricity, telephone, and running water were first installed after the war, when Giacometti came into money. By that time, however, the studio had already become a legendary place by virtue of its almost demonstrative poverty, a symbol of the existential artistic *vie de bohème* per se.

The studio was
something like a stage
for Giacometti.

"Strangely, I thought that this studio was tiny when I rented it 1927. But it was the first opportunity to present itself and I had no choice. I wanted to move out as soon as possible because it was so cramped—it was hardly larger than a hole. But the longer I stayed, the bigger it became. I was able to do everything here," Giacometti said in 1964.[34] The studio was in fact tiny: it was only twenty-three square meters large, or small, to be precise. But it grew into a thought-space solely because Giacometti covered the walls with sketches (ill. pages 72, 80/81). Two drawings of the studio dating from 1932 make it seem enormous. They resemble drawn statements of account with views of the works that were produced or even only conceived in this room. Many of the objects that were intended to represent feeling can be seen there. In a preparatory sketch for the studio drawings that he drew on a blank page of an exhibition catalogue of works by his godfather Cuno

64

Amiet, one can see him as a tiny figure lying in bed surrounded by the nightmare-like figments of his imagination that seemed to overwelm him. Particularly this drawing resembles one of the stage designs he had already made as an adolescent. The studio was in fact something like a stage for Giacometti, who seems to have also been exceptionally gifted at self-promotion, very conscious of his impact and the impact of his working environment on his many visitors and photographers.

In a drawing depicting the studio (ill. pages 66/67), at the center of a three-legged worktable, an object can be seen that would become Giacometti's very first piece to enter a museum collection, namely the Museum of Modern Art in New York in 1936: *Le Palais à quatre heures du matin (The Palace at 4 a.m.)* (ill. page 68, a delicate construction from 1932, comprising small wooden rods standing on a wooden panel, in which figures and small objects are placed. It has a front side and gives the appearance of a stage design. If the studio drawings are retrospectives of the objects conceived in the studio as a thought-space, *Palace* is a kind of studio within a studio portraying the world of thought, the pictures and occurrences that produced all of this, hence making it a kind of self-portrait. The reading experiences of his youth mentioned in the letters addressed to Lucas Lichtenhan are probably also dealt with here. Heinrich Heine's early tragedy *Almansor,* a story from the time of the Christian *Reconquista* of Spain from the Muslims, is full of fantastic descriptions of palaces. Alberto, who had a pseudo-Moorish palace right at his own doorstep in Stampa in the shape of Palazzo Castelmur, read them enthusiastically, as he wrote on April 18, 1918; it is "all like a dream." And one of the main motifs of Goethe's *Wilhelm Meister's Journeyman Years,* which the young Alberto also read, is the arrival of the journeymen in palaces. Alberto's sadistic "falling asleep fantasies" again come to mind here.

But those who wish to at least rudimentarily comprehend what this is all about must read Giacometti's text that supposedly deciphers *Palace:* "We used to construct a fantastic palace at night (days and nights had the same color, as if everything happened just before daybreak; throughout the whole time I never saw the sun), a very fragile palace of matchsticks; at the slightest clumsy movement a whole part of the tiny building would collapse; we always started again. I do not know why it came to be inhabited by a backbone in a cage—the backbone the woman sold me on one of the first nights I met her in the street—and by one of the skeleton birds which she saw the very night before our life together came to an end— the skeleton birds which were hovering in the great unroofed hall high over the basin with clear, green water in which the razor-thin,

65

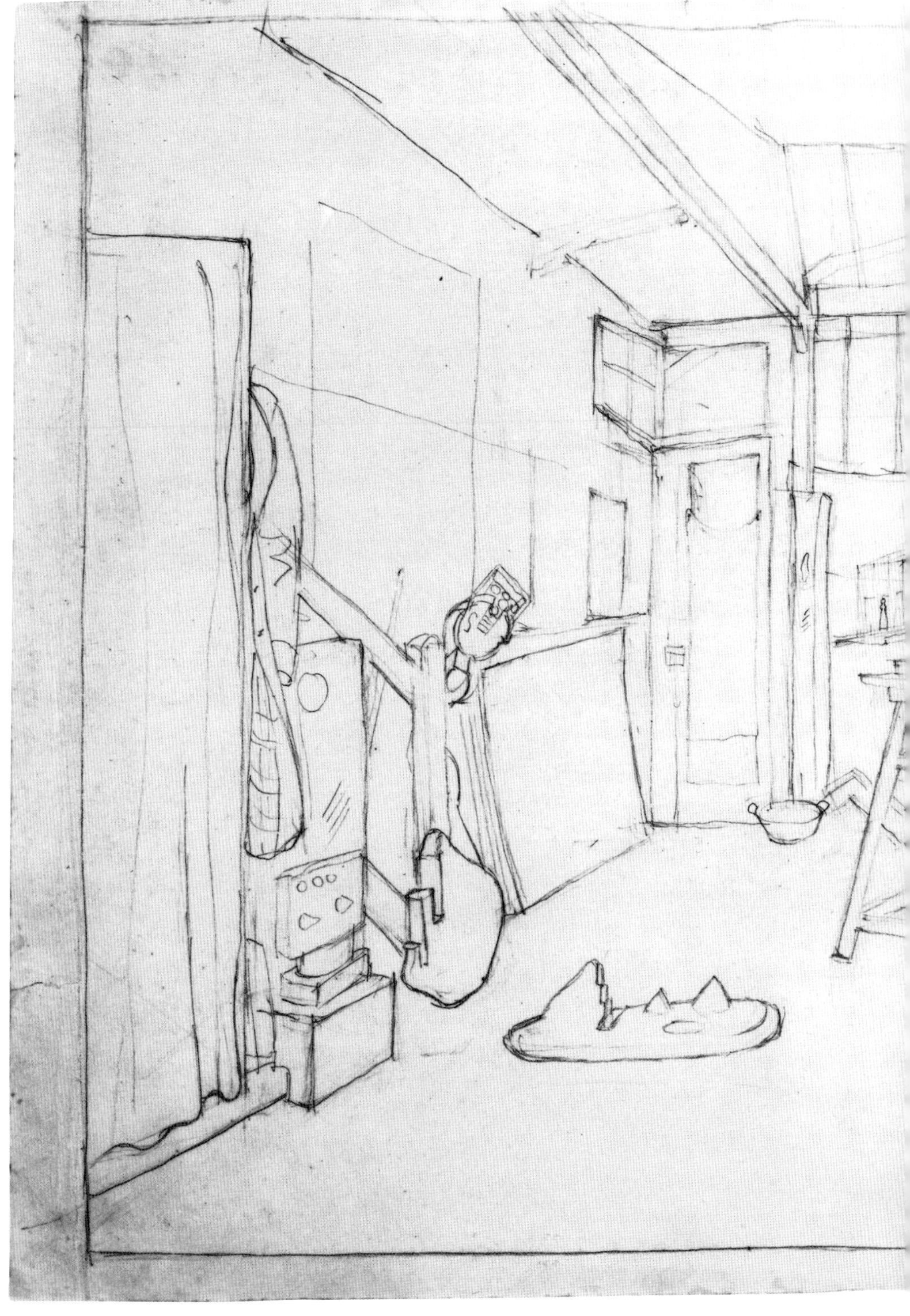

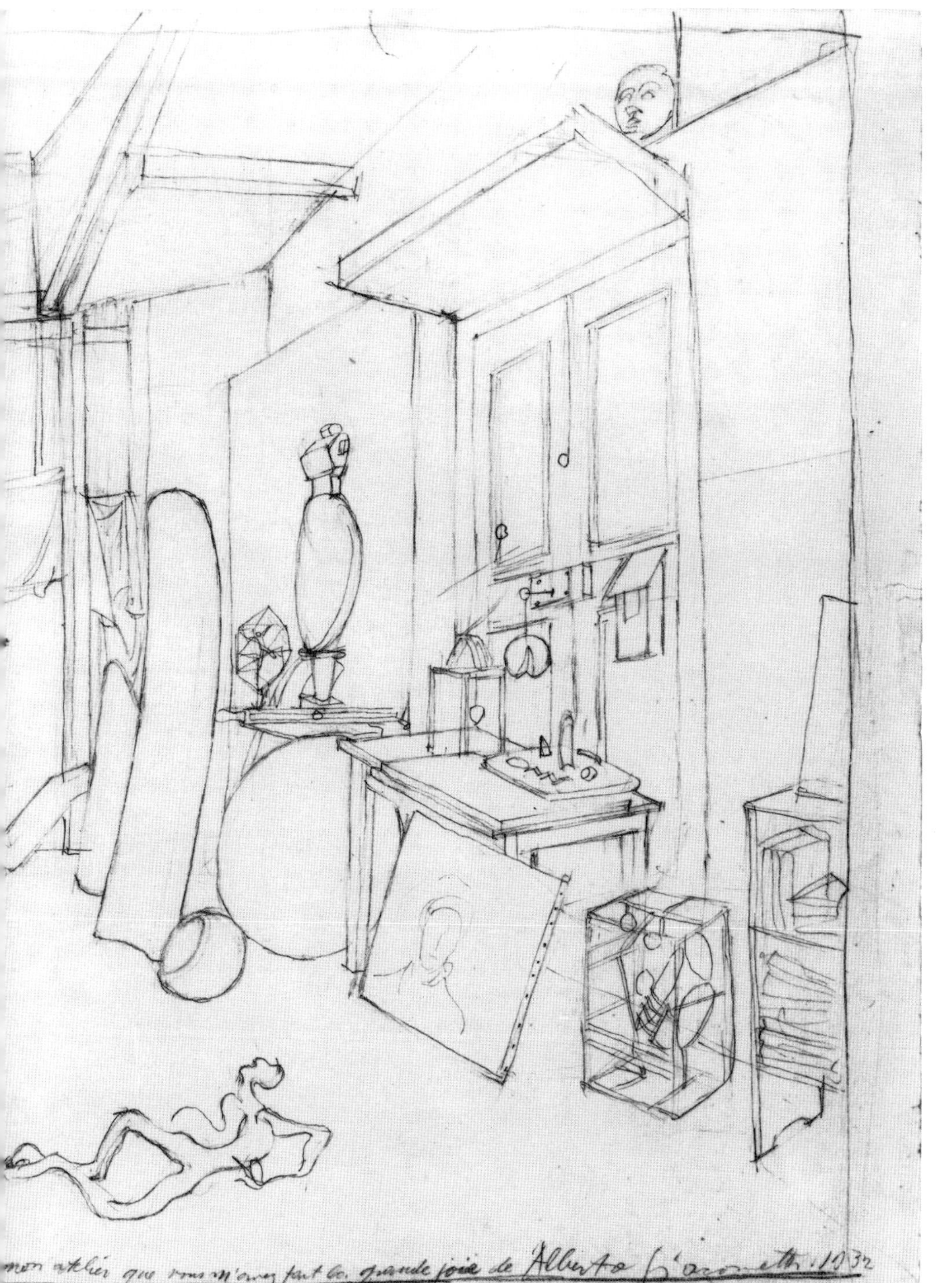

mon atelier que vous m'avez fait la grande joie de   Alberto Giacometti 1932
ne pas trouver détestable.

DESSIN DE MON ATELIER
(STUDIO, AT THE FRONT) 1932
Pencil on vellum paper, 32.7 x 49.3 cm
Kunstmuseum Basel, Kupferstichkabinett

LE PALAIS À 4 HEURES DU MATIN
(THE PALACE AT 4 A.M.) 1932
Photograph by Man Ray
from *Cahiers d'Art* 2/3 (1932)

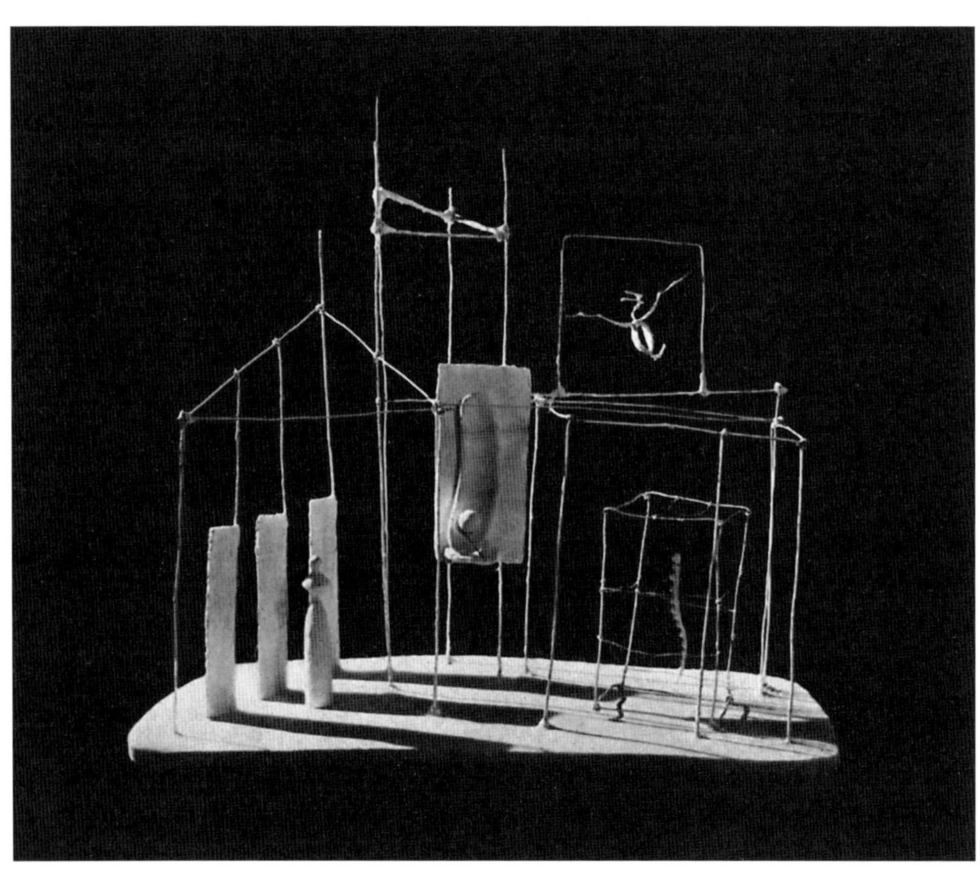

snow-white skeleton birds swam among exclamations of astonishment at four o'clock in the morning. In the middle rose the scaffolding of a tower, its top perhaps unfinished, perhaps fallen in ruin. On the other side there appeared the statue of a woman in which I recognized my mother, just as she impressed me in my earliest memories. The mystery of her long black dress touching the floor troubled me: apparently a part of her body, it frightened and confused me. This figure stands against the same curtain thrice repeated, the very curtain I saw when I opened my eyes for the first time. Fascinated, I fixed my gaze upon this brown curtain beneath which, along the polished floor, filtered a narrow gleam of light. I can say nothing of the red object in front of the board. I identify it with myself."[35]

But *Cube* from 1933, which is also known as *Pavillon nocturne (Nocturnal Pavilion)* (ill. page 53) is the true end point and culmination of this phase in which Giacometti intensely dealt with his emotional sensations since childhood. The plaster version can be seen as a three-dimensional realization of the polyhedron from Dürer's engraving *Melancholy I,* as an extreme geometric reduction and abstraction of reality, or an artifact per se. The "evil" pyramid-like stone from the text "Hier, sables mouvants" again comes to mind here. Giacometti not only described *Cube* as his sole abstract work, but he also called it *Tête,* or "head." The scored self-portrait and the suggestion of a studio in the bronze version of the work turn *Cube* into a kind of crystalline metaphor for Giacometti's artistic personality as expressed by his studio, an extreme from which he set out to approach reality.

For a long time it was possible for Giacometti to depict reality in the form that it presented itself to him only by means of the motion sculptures made "from memory" that were intended to elicit emotions. His separation from the Surrealist group around André Breton in 1935 meant the return to the model for Giacometti. For years he worked on sculptures of heads, whereby he was primarily guided by the model of ancient Egyptian art. Giacometti was driven by the notion of wanting to produce a kind of second reality after nature, but only very few works from these years survived his self-critical glance. Although he spent years in his studio working on the single "correct" head, Giacometti was nevertheless productive, a fact that seems to have been forgotten to some extent—a result of the traditional disdain of the applied arts as opposed to the fine arts. As a designer of fixtures largely for the then very successful interior architect Jean-Michel Frank, Giacometti primarily designed vases and lamps, all in all roughly one hundred objects, whose duplication also occupied his brother Diego. The two brothers earned their living in this way.

Jean-Michel Frank (1895–1941), who rallied a group of artists from the circle of the Surrealists around him about 1930, propagated the *luxe pauvre* style, an "impoverished luxury" consisting of rooms that were sparsely decorated with objects made of seemingly archaic "simple" materials such as plaster and parchment. Giacometti's plaster and terracotta objects, whether painted or unpainted, give the impression of sculptural studies playing with symmetry and multiple views, with regularity and irregularity. Giacometti had characterized his 1933 *Cube* as a head, but also as his sole abstract structure; many objects of daily use from the nineteen-thirties can be regarded as further developments of this abstract sculpture.

His activity for Frank made Giacometti realize that the work of an artist was not fundamentally different from that of a mechanic or an artisan. By his own account, this recognition was behind his decision to continue working after nature, or to take it up again: "One must return to the roots and start all over again."[36] On the other hand, however, this work helped him "see things in their place, in their spatial surroundings."[37] His return to working from the model as well as the definition of objects in space resulting from his activity for Jean-Michel Frank led to a long period of portraying what he described to Pierre Schneider in 1961 as "stable reality" ("une réalité . . . stable").[38]

Stable reality: that is the reality in precisely the form in which it presented itself to Giacometti's perception. This particularly refers to the famous tiny figures (ill. page 72) of which Giacometti took a few when he was supposed to install a sculpture at the 1939 Swiss National Exhibition. They represent figures whose size was determined by the distance between the figure and Giacometti's eyes. In 1937, a crucial year for him in which, at home in his native region, he essentially laid the foundation for his late painting style with his apple still lifes and the portrait of his mother, Giacometti experienced something to which his earliest tiny figures can be traced back. It was like an initial spark for the other small figures: "The sculpture I wanted to make of this woman [his girlfriend Isabel Nicholas] corresponded in reality precisely to the manner in which I saw her before me on the street from a certain distance. I therefore wanted to give it the size that she had when she was at this distance. . . . It was about midnight on Boulevard Saint-Michel. I saw the vast, expansive darkness over her, saw the houses—in order to reproduce my impression, I should have painted a picture and not made a sculpture. Or I could have made an enormous pedestal so that it corresponded to what I saw."[39]

As indicated above, one should not forget to also understand the tiny figures from 1937 as a reaction against the gargantuanism at that year's Paris World's Fair, which could not only be seen in the monumental sculptures so popular in totalitarian states. In his memoirs, the sculptor and painter Hugo Weber (1918–1971) described, albeit in a somewhat poetically exaggerated form, how this not only involved Giacometti's perception, but rather the fundamental question regarding the impact and monumentality of a sculpture. Weber, who lived in Giacometti's neighborhood, met Giacometti in Paris in 1939. He visited him in Geneva, where Giacometti sojourned between 1942 and 1945 when he was not in Maloja or Stampa. The husband of his deceased sister Ottilia lived in Geneva with her son Silvio, whose upbringing was being watched over by his grandmother, Alberto's mother Annetta:

71

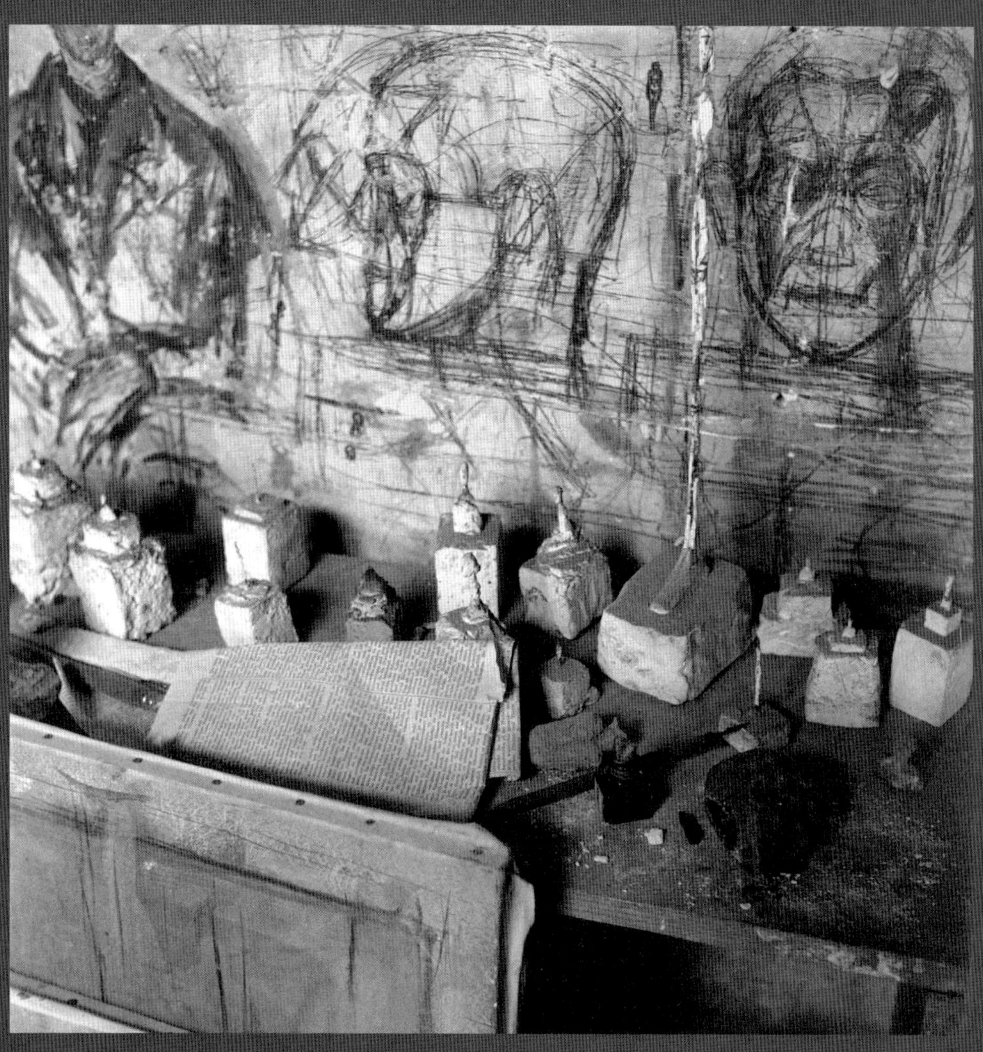

Wall drawing in the Parisian studio,
in front of it the seemingly monumental
tiny figures from the time before 1945

"During the course of our day-long discussion, we had taken a ferry across Lake Geneva to visit Fritz Huf, a sculptor. Having reached the other side of the lake, we gazed back at the lake from our vantage point on the pier. Looking far out, to the very end of the adjoining public beach, amazingly we both saw the same thing at the same time: a figure, or rather the essence of a female figure, bathed in sunlight. Whether this was an illusion caused by the light on the water, or whether it was something created by our imagination and the force of our conversation, I do not know. In any case, we viewed this "pin," and while we realized that this was not, in fact, a pin, to our eyes it had the dimensions of a pin. Even more intriguing than that already discussed, this object was a study in contradictions: simultaneously smaller than a solitary pin and yet bigger than Mont Blanc, which rose majestically behind it. The vastness of the horizontal lake and the immense height of the vertical mountain surrounding the tiny figure did not reduce the figure's importance. On the contrary, it emphasized it."[40]

It is perhaps not coincidental that Giacometti and Weber had this experience in conjunction with a visit to the now largely forgotten Fritz Huf (1888–1970). He first became known with his figurative sculptures and portrait busts in the style of Georg Kolbe and Hermann Haller. Huf began masking abstract objects in the early nineteen-thirties and in Paris became a member of the Abstraction-Création group, to which Giacometti was also close. Weber, who was later an important Abstract Expressionist artist in the United States, began his career as a student of Aristide Maillol, the creator of voluptuous idealized sculptures of women.

TIME AND SPACE

Giacometti was first able to free himself from his compulsion to diminutiveness at the moment when he discovered a satisfactory artistic solution to the problem of depicting the continuum of time and space. In his perhaps most famous, but also most puzzling text, "Le rêve, le sphinx et la mort de T.," published in 1946 in the magazine *Labyrinthe,* Giacometti evocatively described his outlook on this matter; it is quoted here again: "Suddenly I had the feeling that every event existed simultaneously around me. Time became horizontal and circular, was simultaneously space, and I tried to draw it."[41] Giacometti not only addressed his feelings about the congruence of time and space here. In his "Notes sur les copies" written in 1965 for the magazine *L'Éphémère* where he emphasized the significance of copying for his work, he wrote: "All the art of the past, of all epochs and cultures, rises up before me, all simultaneously, as if space had taken the place of time."[42]

The subject was omnipresent in modern art, particularly in contemporary Bauhaus-influenced architecture.[43] Albert Einstein's recently published theory of relativity, whose essential component is the concept of space-time, led to misunderstandings among artists. These may be a consequence of the fact that theoretical physics proceeds from the idea of absolute space as set forth by Newton, while artists tend to view space as defined by bodies, i.e., "that it is only the reciprocal relationship of bodies that 'unfolds' space," as Leibniz postulated.[44] This is also indicated in a note written by Giacometti circa 1949 in which he denied the existence of absolute space: "Space does not exist, you have to create it, but it does not exist, no."[45]

Giacometti had occupied himself long before 1946 with the question of representing reality as time and space, long before he became acquainted—probably through Simone de Beauvoir—with

74

the writings of Maurice Merleau-Ponty, particularly his 1945 book *La phénoménologie de la perception (The Phenomenology of Perception)*. Merleau-Ponty is readily seen in conjunction with Giacometti, although there was probably no such clear description of the congruence between time and space in his works as there is in Giacometti's.

One can already read in the letters to Lucas Lichtenhan how intensely Giacometti felt time. On May 29, 1918, he wrote that he saw memories as a "huge picture behind you," and one is also reminded of his text "Le rêve, le sphinx et la mort de T." where Giacometti writes: "I do not understand why, but I lived completely in my recollections. Everything I saw, the most insignificant trifles, reminded me of something. I now saw myself here, now there, once in Schiers, then suddenly as a small child at home, then in my father's studio, etc. I remember how I sat near my father in the gray past, almost in prehistoric times, and drew."

Time and space
become as one.

That the young Giacometti already saw time and space as a single entity is also demonstrated in his mention of a space "in which time forgot the hour" in his 1933 text "Charbon d'herbe."[46] These ideas were very tangible for Giacometti. In "Le rêve, le sphinx et la mort de T." he attempted to draw them as a disc composed of segments circumscribed by stelae. He could move about on this disc in his imagination, or, strictly speaking, through time and space.

Where Giacometti could have found the inspiration for his ideas can only be suggested here; in any case it was surely not only from such physics theoreticians and space-time specialists as Hermann Minkowski or even Albert Einstein. The best known and most popular mention of the congruency between time and space before Minkowski occurs in Richard Wagner's opera *Parsifal,* which was premiered in 1882. At the conclusion of the first act, there is an exchange between the innocent "pure fool" Parsifal and his wise mentor Gurnemanz, which in Lionel Salter's 1970 translation reads as follows: Parsifal. "I scarcely tread, yet seem already to come far." Gurnemanz. "You see, my son, here time becomes space."

Wagner's source was probably Arthur Schopenhauer's *Die Welt als Wille und Vorstellung (The World as Will and Representation),* where similar thoughts can be found even though Schopenhauer believed that music was one of the arts that unfolds chronologically, but not spatially; Wagner probably wanted to prove Schopenhauer wrong in his *Parsifal*. Giacometti was already familiar with Schopenhauer as a sixteen year old; on May 3, 1918, he mentions him in a letter to Lucas Lichtenhan. It is not known, however, if he had ever seen *Parsifal*.

But Alberto had in fact indicated that he was enthusiastic about the German Romantic writers as a boy. Seemingly very modern statements can be found, for example, in Novalis' fragments, such as "Space is enduring time—time is fluid, variable space" or "A permeated space is a time-space. A permeated time—a space-time." But here too, it is doubtful if Giacometti was familiar with Novalis' philosophical fragments. If one follows the descriptions written by the young artist Alberto in his letters to Lucas Lichtenhan, he must have identified to a certain extent with Gottfried Keller's *Der Grüne Heinrich (Green Henry)*, who experiences the world while wandering across it. It is also certain that he knew Goethe's writings. The structure of Goethe's late work *Wilhelm Meisters Wanderjahre (Wilhelm Meister's Journeyman Years)*, which Giacometti had read, is defined by the notion of wandering through the world and the related antipode of staying in place, an idea that is also at the core of works such as the various versions of *Homme qui marche (Walking Man)* and *Femme debout (Standing Woman)* (ill. pages 8/9, back cover). It is very probable that he was also familiar with Goethe's poems from the *Sturm und Drang* period. Goethe's most impressive evocation of the unity of space and time is the poem *An Schwager Kronos,* written "in the mail coach on October 10, 1774," in which the deity Cronus is equated with Chronos, the personification of time. The events run like a film past the clattering and jolting mail coach, the center of the experience where the poetry-writing hero repeatedly spurs the coachman on to ride faster. Time and space become as one and like all the examples mentioned here, they are joined to each other by motion.

Back to Giacometti's drawing of a space-time disc in his text "Le rêve, le sphinx et la mort de T." from 1946, which has various precursors in his work. It recalls a drawing he made as a child between 1912 and 1915 showing an iconographically extremely unusual simultaneous representation of the events described in the fifth chapter of the Book of Revelation and culminating in the adoration of the Lamb by the twenty-four elders and the symbols of the four evangelists. Alberto was naturally familiar with images that spatially represented sequences of time from the illustrations made by his father for the fairy tales from the Engadin region of Switzerland compiled by Gian Bundi in 1901 as a succession of images accompanying the text in a picture frieze. For his disc drawing of the space-time continuum, Giacometti was conceivably able to return to a pictorial invention of

76

youth because by 1946 he had succeeded in reconciling his perception of reality with the possibility of portraying motion. While "stable reality" previously revolved in relationship to himself at the zero point of a strictly three-dimensional coordinate system of his perception, he now succeeded in adding the aspect of time, as manifested in motion, to adequately visualize the four-dimensional space-time.

Two examples suffice to demonstrate what happened. There is a famous photograph that can be seen as a kind of test assembly. Giacometti surely had a direct influence on what the photographs were to show. The original plaster cast of *Femme au chariot (Woman with Chariot)*, dated by Véronique Wiesinger to around 1945 and probably an idealized portrait of his girlfriend Isabel, is visible in front of the nearly life-sized picture of a standing woman Giacometti had painted on the wall of his Majola studio. The scene is "guarded" by his father's plaster mask (ill. page 78). The chariot—supposedly a toy once owned by his nephew Silvio—on which the figure stands is crucial. One could almost say that the plastic figure had detached itself from the wall, as if it had driven directly out of it. A figure that can be moved because it stands on wheels makes the distance between itself, as object, and the perceiving self, i.e., Giacometti, variable. The dictates of fixed distance have been overcome.

"... I experienced
motion as a
sequence of stills."

A further event was decisive in order for Giacometti to break through to his "classic" works of the postwar period. Alberto himself described it numerous times, perhaps most succinctly in his 1961 conversation with Pierre Schneider. A film he had seen at the movies inspired him to see motion as a sequence of stills: "My view had changed from that moment on; I experienced motion as a succession of stills. A person who was speaking was no longer a person who moved; it was non-motions instead that followed each other one by one and which were all clearly isolated from the others. They were stills that could have lasted an eternity and which were replaced by stills of the same type. I recall that I once ordered something in a café and that the waiter moved his mouth and said something, and that I experienced these movements of his mouth as a sequence of motionless moments each standing perfectly on their own and unrelated to the next one. In this way, the human being became something completely unknown, became a mechanism."[47]

77

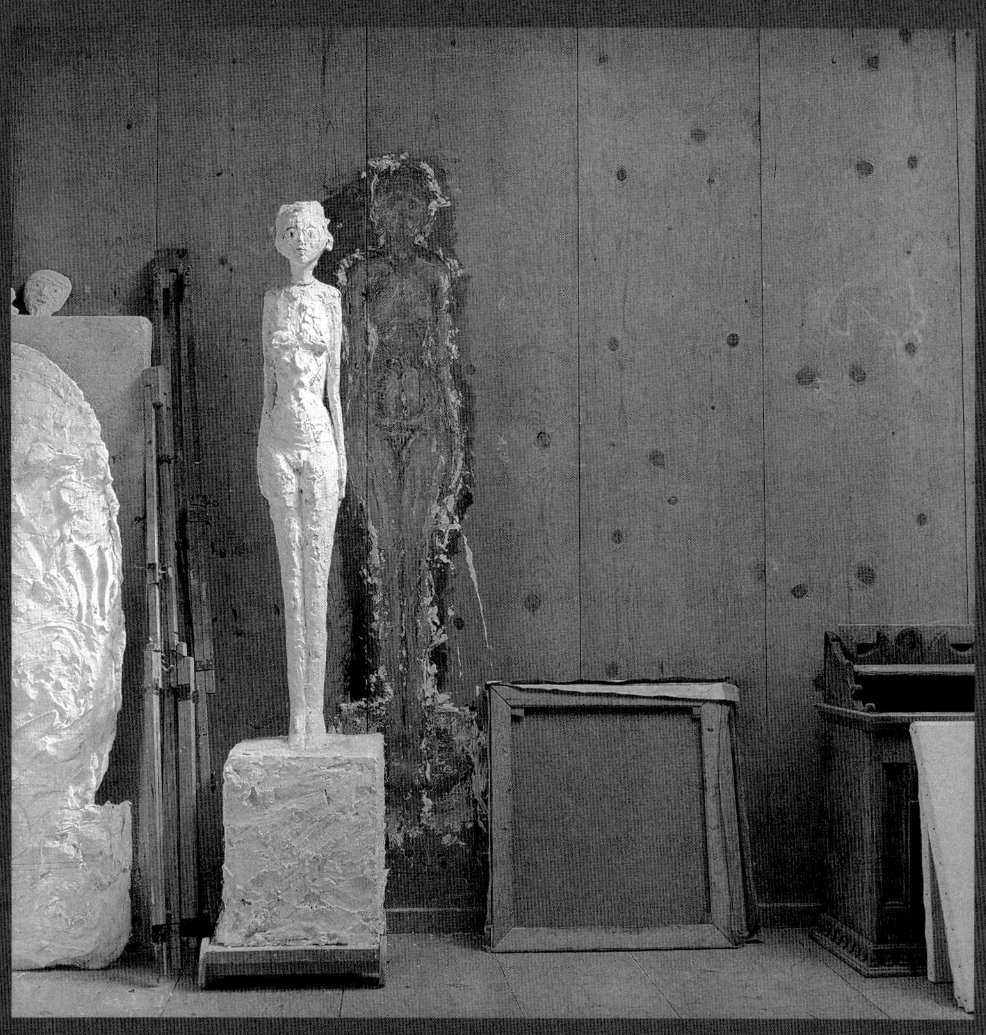

The studio in Maloja after 1950:
the plaster of *Femme au chariot*
(Woman with Chariot),
a standing nude on the wall,
and at the left the grotesque mask of his father

78

Motion as a succession of stills: it is amazing that four-dimensional space-time is also explained by theoretical physics with very similar words.[48] Portraying one of these stills by itself means having found a means to capture it as a part of a whole motion sequence. This is decisive for the reception of the Giacometti's works after 1945. The reality of motion is portrayed in them; time and space become as one. The late frontal portraits as well as the sculptures of heads are manifestations of the human being as a complete stranger, whose essential reality entails being a part of a motion sequence unfolding spatially as well as chronologically. For Giacometti, individuality expresses itself solely in the sitter's glance. The incorporeal, emblematic nature of the sculptures as well as the roughened and therefore imprecisely comprehended nature of their surface and contour underscore the fact that standstill is a fleeting moment.

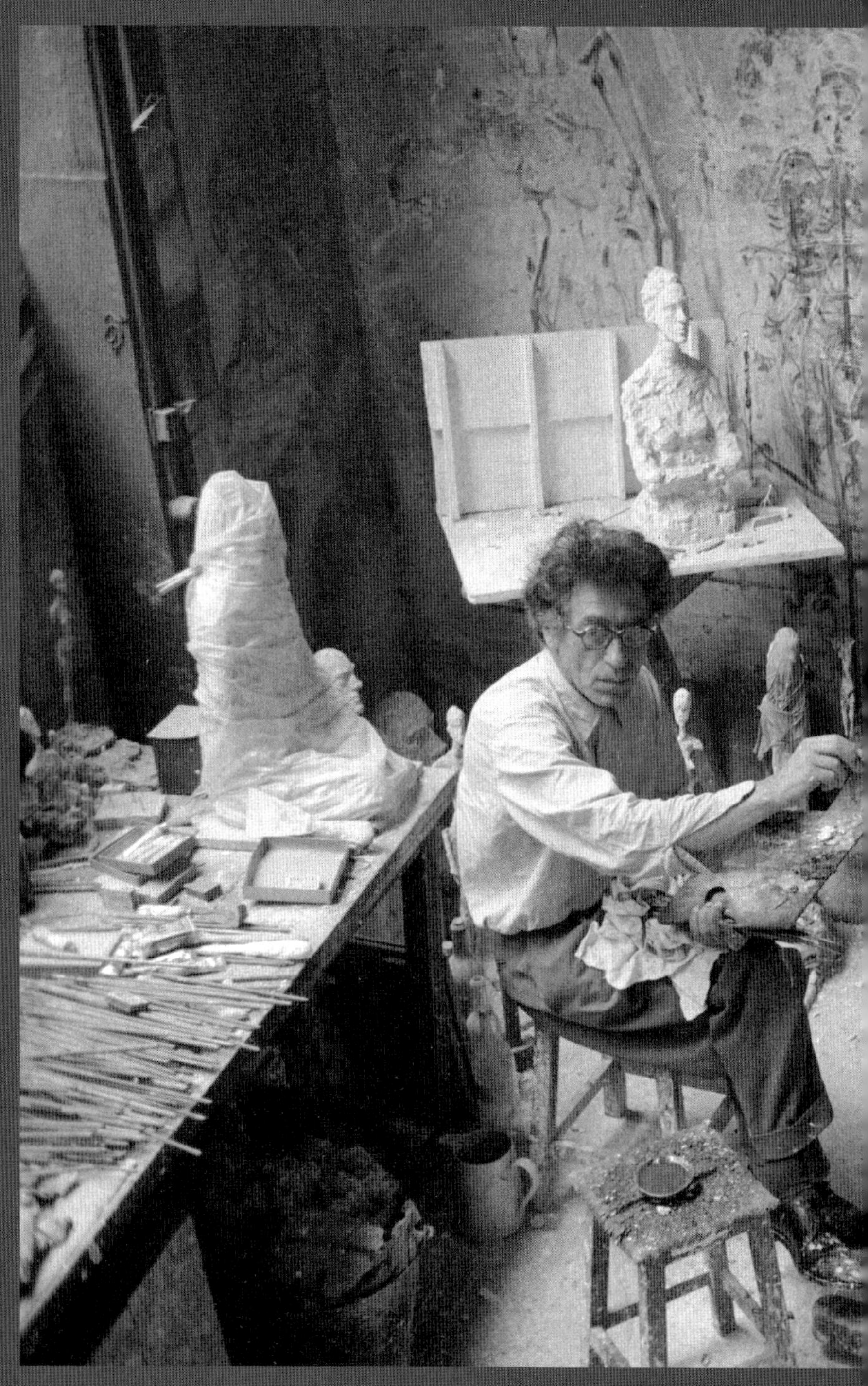

Painting in the Parisian studio, ca. 1960

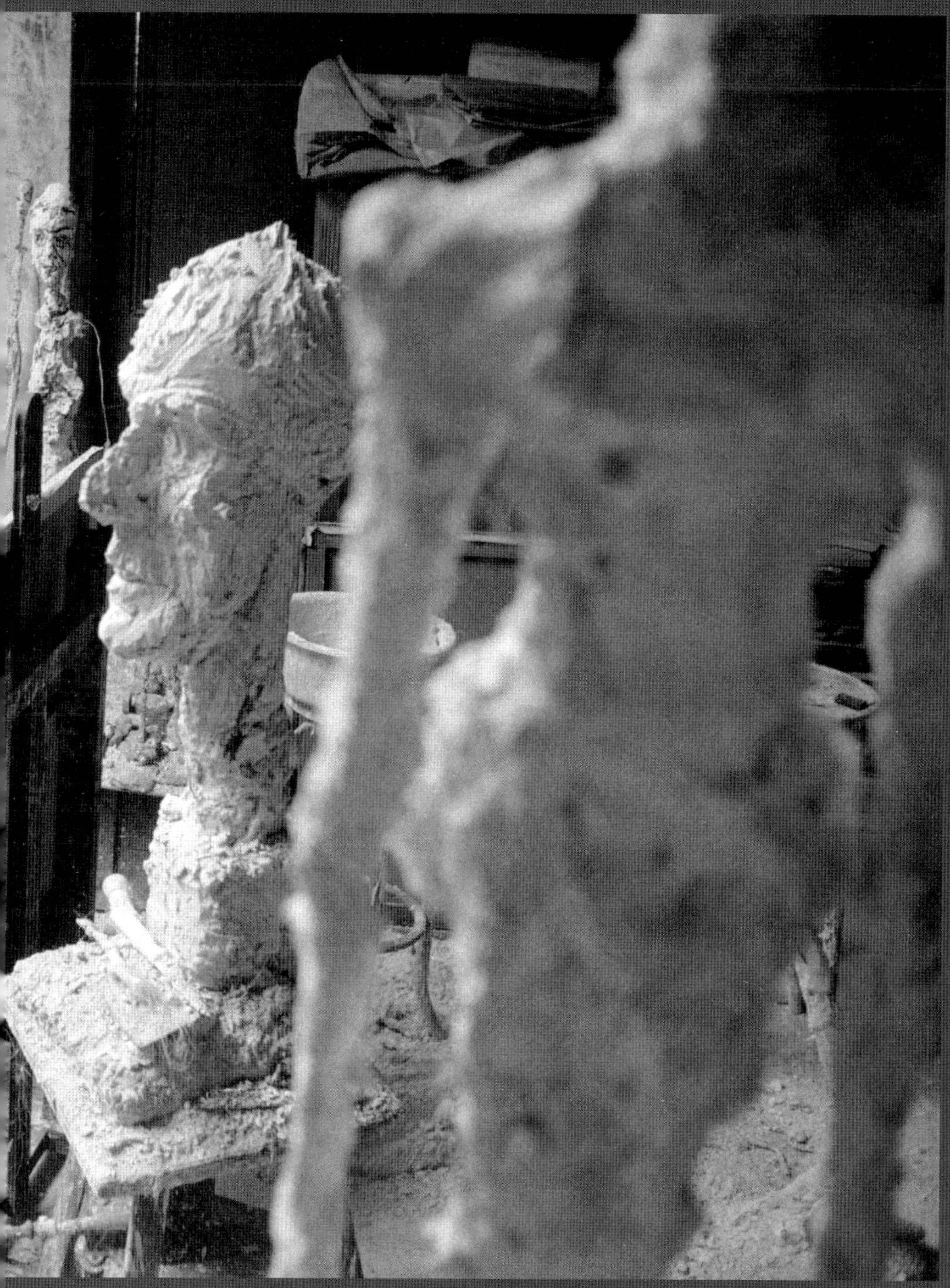

EPILOGUE

Late November 1965: Giacometti had reached the zenith of his fame during his own lifetime. The world's most important museums organized retrospective exhibitions and began intensely collecting his works. Over the course of these years, he himself visited the exhibitions at the Tate Gallery in London, the Museum of Modern Art in New York, and the Louisiana Museum of Modern Art near Copenhagen. In New York he was greatly occupied with the project of erecting a group of figures on Chase Manhattan Plaza (ill. pages 8/9). He finally received the acknowledgment he deserved in Switzerland. After a long back and forth, the Giacometti Foundation was established in Zurich, the core of its collection formed by works previously owned by the American steel magnate G. David Thompson. Giacometti added to them with a number of donations. Bern University presented him an honorary doctorate. He spent three intense days in Bern as Eberhard Kornfeld's guest before taking the night train back to Paris, where he arrived on the morning of November 30. Giacometti had become a living legend. Helène Grob, who was then a secretary at the Kunsthaus Zürich, recalls that as a young person one looked up to him admiringly; one projected one's own wishes and desires onto his striking personality.

Giacometti sought out a doctor on December 1. He had already complained about discomfort while still Bern, particularly about his chronic cough. He was afraid that the cancer for which he had been operated on in 1963 was returning. The doctor reassured, but advised him to have himself thoroughly examined in a hospital. Giacometti decided to be admitted to the largest hospital in his native region, the Kantonsspital in Chur. He left Paris on December 5. He felt alright at first in Chur, and he could even work. But then his condition rapidly deteriorated. He died on January 11, 1966, and was buried in his native village on January 15. Guests came to the funeral from far and near. The cause of death was pericarditis and an associated cardiac infarction brought on by chronic bronchitis. Giacometti, a chain smoker and night worker, had been gambling with his health for years. Nowadays, one would say that he suffered a massive burnout; at least that is the way that the reports by friends shocked about his condition can be interpreted.

Even before Giacometti traveled to Chur, Ernst Scheidegger had come to Paris to speak to him about the commentary for the film he had made with the cameraman and film editor Peter Münger: this cinematic portrait of Giacometti is one of the great artist documentary films of the twentieth century and stands on equal footing with Hans Namuth's Jackson Pollock films and Henri-Georges Clouzot's *Le mystère Picasso.*

"He kneaded, hollowed, squeezed, and stroked the clay."

Scheidegger, who had been friends with Giacometti since 1943, was able to film the artist while he sculpted and painted. He probably did not need a long time to talk Giacometti into doing it, because on the one hand there had already been earlier, albeit less explicit attempts to approach Giacometti's work cinematically, and on the other Giacometti was very responsive to the media of film. Film comprises a sequence of stills, making it an exemplary model for the presentation of motion that Giacometti had attempted to realize. The artist had probably already spoken with his father about the potentials of cinema. After returning home from a visit to his son in Paris in 1930, Giovanni wrote that in his recollection his impressions of Paris were like a combination of film and reality and that he now wanted to paint "a kind of cinematographic landscape."[49] Scheidegger is the author of some of the best descriptions of Giacometti's working methods; they can be followed in the film:

"Alberto had fine, beautiful, sensitive hands, and one could be captivated for hours on end watching how they glided up and down a figure, shaped a head, and kneaded everything back together in order to shape it again. He kneaded, hollowed, squeezed, and stroked the clay. From time to time he rendered the eyes precisely with the knife, kneaded everything together again, poked a bit around the nose, in order to reanimate the head."[50]

It is also impressive to observe in the film how Giacometti's glance moves back and forth between the sitter and the

83

painting, how on his path towards his goal of representating an exaggerated reality, he regularly seeks the inspiration emanating from the sitter. In the film he starts the portrait of Jacques Dupin, the author of the 1962 monograph designed by Scheidegger. To use Ernst Scheidegger's words, one can see "how an picture comes about, how a portrait is constructed on a white canvas, how it grows from the eyes, and how the structure arises, applied with a brush, a painted drawing, in fact, that then takes on color."

The film clearly demonstrates again that his works and all the pieces produced while he was working were parts of an ongoing process that was continued on a yet higher level. Giacometti was constantly on the path to an unattainable perfection, whereby the individual piece is by all means complete in and of itself and can stand entirely on its own. In the development of his art, there is progress as motion as well as persistence as departure point of development—that is, that which characterizes his work.

Perhaps the viewer has finally begun to understand Giacometti's enigmatic character and work when he asks himself the following during an encounter with the artist's sculptures and paintings: am I moving, or is it the figures?

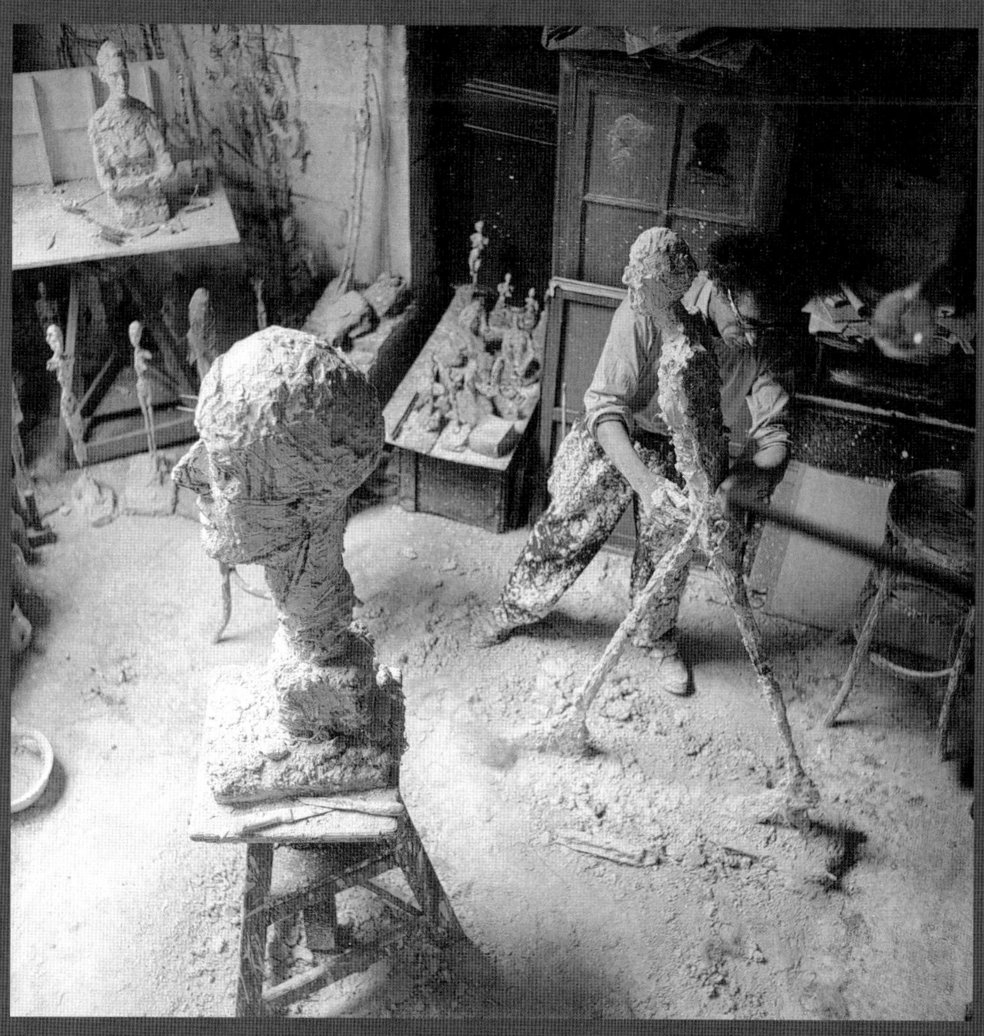

Working on the plaster version of
Homme qui marche, ca. 1960

This book is dedicated to all witnesses to history
who keep their reminiscences alive
and share them with following generations.

Of the countless books and essays written about Alberto Giacometti,
these were particularly helpful to me:

Hohl, Reinhold. *Alberto Giacometti.* Stuttgart, 1971.
———. *Giacometti: Eine Bildbiographie.* Ostfildern-Ruit, 1998. (Translated as *Giacometti: A Biography in Pictures.* Ostfildern-Ruit, 1998.)
Scheidegger, Ernst. *Spuren einer Freundschaft: Alberto Giacometti.* 2nd rev. ed. Zurich and Frankfurt a. M., 2000. (Translated as *Traces of a Friendship: Alberto Giacometti.* Rev. ed. Zurich, 2006.) (Photographs and texts)
Alberto Giacometti. Edited by Christian Klemm. Exh. cat. Kunsthaus Zürich; The Museum of Modern Art, New York. Berlin, 2001.
L'atelier d'Alberto Giacometti: Collection de la Fondation Alberto et Annette Giacometti. Edited by Véronique Wiesinger. Exh. cat. Centre Pompidou. Paris, 2007.

1   The letters written in German by Alberto Giacometti to Lucas Lichtenhan are preserved in the Alberto Giacometti Foundation, Zurich.
2   Translated from Alberto Giacometti, *Écrits: Articles, notes et entretiens,* ed. Fondation Alberto et Annette Giacometti (hereafter abbreviated FAAG) (Paris, 2008), p. 599.
3   Translated from Donat Rütimann, ed., *Alberto Giacometti: Le rêve, le sphinx et la mort de T. / Der Traum, die Sphinx und der Tod von T.* (Zurich, 2005), p. 126.
4   Translated from Reinhold Hohl, ed., *Giacometti: Eine Bildbiographie* (Ostfildern-Ruit, 1998), p. 7.
5   Translated from Viola Radlach, ed., *Cuno Amiet–Giovanni Giacometti: Briefwechsel* (Zurich, 2000), p. 457.
6   Ibid., p. 348.
7   Véronique Wiesinger, *Giacometti: La figure au défi* (Paris, 2007), p. 108.

8   Translated from Hohl 1998 (see note 4), pp. 17–18.

9   Ibid., p. 96.

10   Undated letter from Alberto Giacometti to his mother, Alberto Giacometti Foundation, Zurich.

11   Translated from the letter in the FAAG, Paris.

12   Translated from Viola Radlach, ed., *Giovanni Giacometti: Briefwechsel mit seinen Eltern, Freunden und Sammlern* (Zurich, 2003), pp. 627–28.

13   Translated from Mary Lisa Palmer and François Chaussende, eds., *Alberto Giacometti: Gestern, Flugsand: Schriften,* 2nd ed. (Zurich, 2006), pp. 116–17. This publication has not been authorized by the FAAG.

14   See Christian Klemm and Dietrich Wildung, *Giacometti, der Ägypter,* exh. cat., Kunsthaus Zürich (2008), p. 48.

15   See Dieter Schwarz, "Giovanni Giacometti – Leben und Werk," in *Giovanni Giacometti 1868–1933,* exh. cat. Kunstmuseum Winterthur (Winterthur, 1996), p. 178.

16   Translated from Hohl 1998 (see note 4), p. 17.

17   Translated from Radlach 2000 (see note 5), p. 560.

18   Translated from Giacometti 2008 (see note 2), p. 310.

19   Translated from Hohl 1998 (see note 4), p.16.

20   Ibid.

21   Translated from Palmer and Chaussende 2006 (see note 13), p. 133.

22   Translated from Schwarz 1996 (see note 15), p. 178.

23   Translated from the letter dated May 29, 1918, Alberto Giacometti Foundation, Zurich.

24   Translated from Schwarz 1996 (see note 15), p. 174.

25   Alberto Giacometti, quoted in David Sylvestor, *Looking at Giacometti* (New York, 1994), p. 26.

26   Translated from Palmer and Chaussende 2006 (see note 13), p. 181.

27   Ibid., pp. 33–35.

28   Translated from Giacometti 2008 (see note 2), p. 311.

29   Ibid., pp. 63–65.

30   Translated from Palmer and Chaussende 2006 (see note 13), letter pp. 62–89, here p. 70. The letter is reproduced in Giacometti 2008 (see note 2), pp. 86–93.

31   Translated from Hohl 1998 (see note 4), pp. 57–58.

32   Christian Klemm, *Alberto Giacometti,* exh. cat. Kunsthaus Zürich; The Museum of Modern Art, New York (Berlin, 2001), p. 74.

33   Translated from Hohl 1998 (see note 4), p. 65.

34   Ibid., p. 50.

35   Translated from Palmer and Chaussende 2006 (see note 13), pp. 42–44.

36   Alberto Giacometti, interview by André Parinaud, 1962, translated from Giacometti 2008 (see note 2), p. 242.

37   Alberto Giacometti, interview by Yvon Taillandier, 1951, translated from Giacometti 2008 (see note 2), pp. 242, 175.

38   Translated from Giacometti 2008 (see note 2), pp. 228–37, here p. 233.

39 Alberto Giacometti, interview by Pierre Dumayet, 1963, translated from Palmer and Chaussende 2006 (see note 13), p. 275.

40 Hugo Weber, "Thinking Back to Alberto Giacometti," edited and annotated by Cathleen H. Bracksmayer in Tamara S. Evans, *Alberto Giacometti and America* (New York, 1984), pp. 24–34, here pp. 29–30.

41 Translated from Giacometti in Rütimann 2005 (see note 3).

42 Translated from Palmer and Chaussende (see note 13), p. 133.

43 See Ulrich Müller, *Raum, Bewegung und Zeit im Werk von Walter Gropius und Ludwig Mies van der Rohe* (Berlin, 2004).

44 Hubert Goenner, *Einsteins Relativitätstheorien: Raum, Zeit, Masse, Gravitation,* 5th ed. (Munich, 2005), p. 9.

45 Translated from Giacometti 2008 (see note 2), p. 542.

46 Translated from Palmer and Chaussende (see note 13), p. 32.

47 Ibid., pp. 259–60.

48 See Norbert Dragon, Institut für Theoretische Physik: "Geometrie der Relativitätstheorie," http://www.itp.uni-hannover.de/ffdragon/Group.html (accessed February 2009), p. 4.

49 Quoted from Véronique Wiesinger, "Giovanni and Alberto Giacometti: Father and Son," in *Giacometti,* exh. cat. Fondation Beyeler (Ostfildern, 2009), pp. 19–25, here p. 25.

50 Translated from Ernst Scheidegger, *Spuren einer Freundschaft: Alberto Giacometti,* 2nd rev. ed. (Zurich and Frankfurt a. M., 2000), p. 157, with the subsequent quote from p. 155.

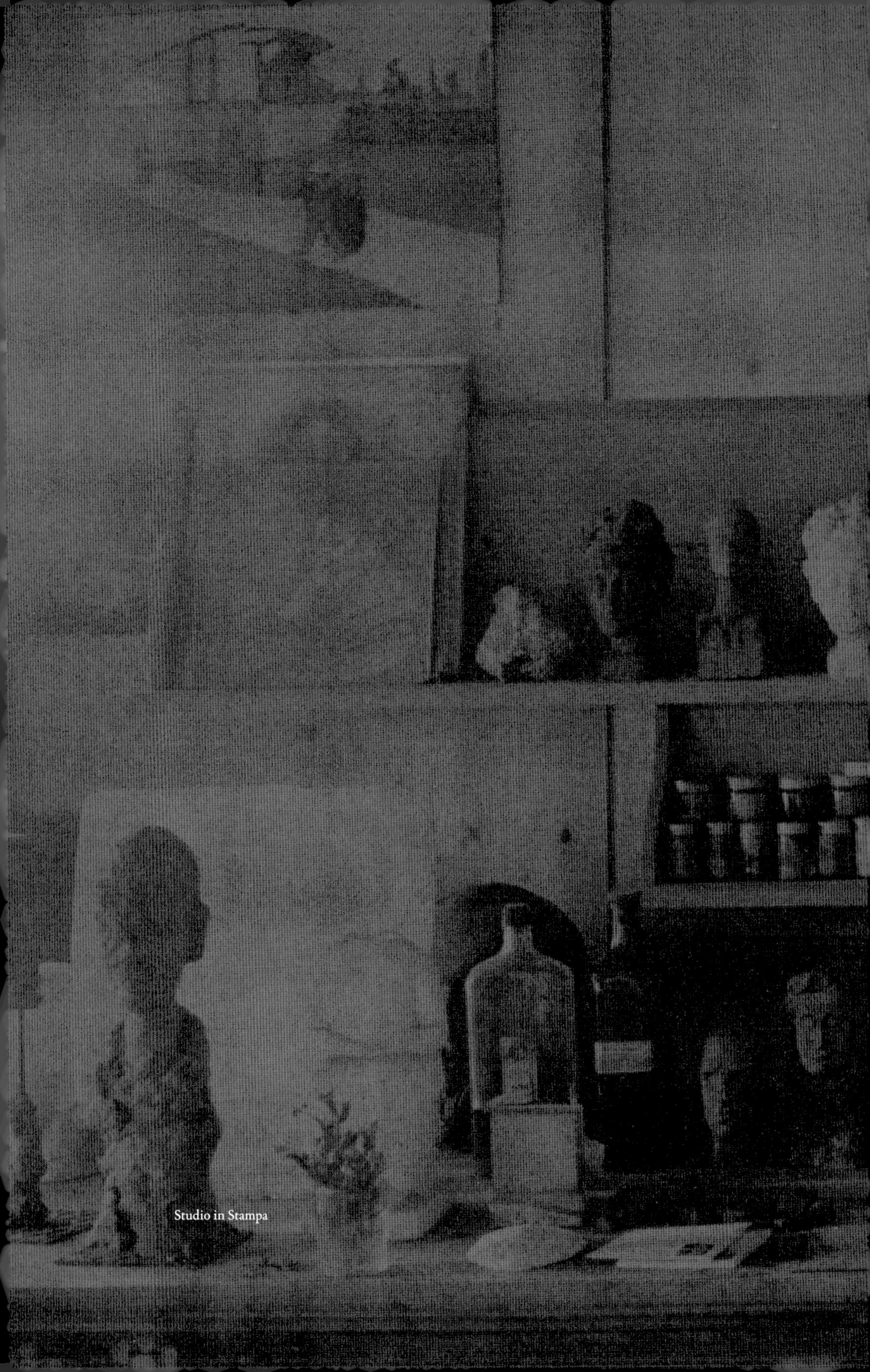
Studio in Stampa

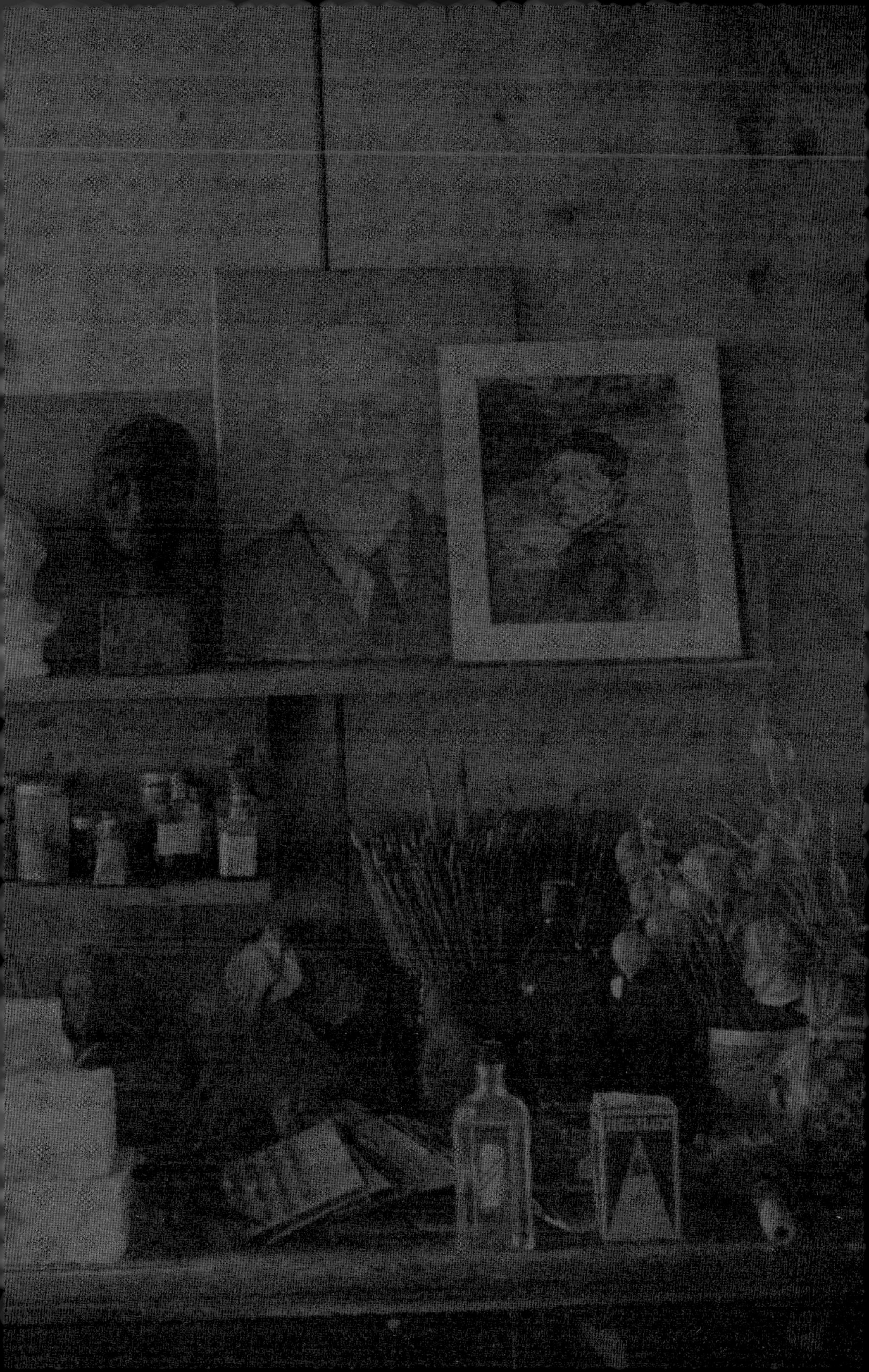

1901   Alberto Giacometti is born on October 10 in Borgonovo near Stampa in the Swiss Val
        Bregaglia. His father Giovanni Giacometti (1868–1933) is an important Post-Impressionist
        painter and printmaker and Alberto's first and most important teacher. His mother is
        Annetta, née Stampa (1871–1964). Alberto has three siblings: Diego (1902–1985), who
        later becomes his most important model and assistant; Ottilia (1904–1937), who dies
        giving birth to her son Silvio; and Bruno (born 1907), who would become an architect.

1906   The family moves to Stampa. Alberto will regularly return to the house on the main street,
        with the stables that were converted into the studio, as well as to the summerhouse in
        Maloja owned by the family since 1910.

1915–19 Attends the cantonal school in Schiers.

1919   Attends the École des Beaux-Arts and the École des Arts et Métiers in Geneva.

1920–21 Travels with his father to Venice. They subsequently stay in Rome and visit Florence, Assisi,
        and Naples.

1922–26 Studies in the class of Antoine Bourdelle at the Académie de la Grande Chaumière in Paris.

1929–35 Disc sculptures such as *Tête qui regarde (Gazing Head)* are followed by moving objects
        such as *Boule suspendue (Suspended Ball)* which make him famous in the avant-garde,
        particularly with the Surrealists, with whom he is close until 1935.

1930   His brother Diego moves permanently to Paris. Start of his work as a designer of articles
        for everyday use for the interior decorator Jean-Michel Frank.

1933   Death of his father on June 25. Albert settles his estate.

1937   Birth of his nephew on October 10. His sister Ottilia dies the next day. Alongside regularly
        discarded representations of heads, he produces his first tiny sculptures and a few
        oil paintings that point the way to his late painting style.

1942–45 Stays in Geneva and Val Bregaglia because he cannot return to Nazi-occupied Paris.
        He meets Annette Arm in 1943. She becomes his favorite model, and they marry in 1949.
        Back in Paris, he intensifies his friendship with Simone de Beauvoir and Jean-Paul Sartre,
        among others.

1946–51 Development of the style that would make him famous: through his experience of motion
        as a succession of stills, his rod-like figures develop into spatial symbols.

1951–56   He starts making sculptures with greater volume while making a series of works after his
           brother Diego's head. First exhibition with Aimé Maeght, his most important art dealer
           alongside Pierre Matisse, goes on show in 1951. Produces the *Femmes de Venise* series.
           He searches for a figure of a woman for his exhibition in the French Pavilion at the Venice
           Biennale. Nine attempts are cast in bronze.

   1956   The Japanese philosophy professor Isaku Yanaihara starts modeling for him, confronting
           the artist with his non-European facial features. They make him uncertain, but his
           portrayal leads the way to his intense late portraits.

   1958   Encounter with "Caroline," a young woman from the Parisian underworld who sits for him
           from 1960.

1959–60   Works on designs for a group of figures intended for installation on Chase Manhattan Plaza
           in New York.

   1962   Grand Prize for Sculpture at the Venice Biennale. Comprehensive retrospective exhibition
           at the Kunsthaus Zürich.

   1964   Death of his mother on January 25. Dedication of the Giacometti galleries and courtyards
           at the Fondation Maeght in Saint-Paul de Vence.

   1965   Travels to retrospective exhibitions of his works: London (Tate Gallery), New York
           (The Museum of Modern Art), and Humlebæk (Louisiana Museum of Modern Art).
           Establishment of the Alberto Giacometti Foundation in Zurich on December 16.

   1966   Alberto Giacometti dies in the cantonal hospital in Chur on January 11. He is buried on
           January 15 in the cemetery of Borgonovo near Stampa.

93